Making Romantic Fabric-Covered Boxes

*This box holds
my treasures dear,
which I've collected
both far and near.*

Making Romantic Fabric-Covered Boxes

Mary Jo Hiney

Sterling Publishing Co., Inc. New York
A Sterling/Chapelle Book

Chapelle Ltd.

Owner: Jo Packham

Design/layout Editor: Leslie Ridenour

Staff: Marie Barber, Ann Bear, Areta Bingham, Kass Burchett, Rebecca Christensen, Holly Fuller, Marilyn Goff, Shirley Heslop, Holly Hollingsworth, Shawn Hsu, Susan Jorgensen, Leslie Liechty, Pauline Locke, Ginger Mikkelsen, Barbara Milburn, Linda Orton, Karmen Quinney, Rhonda Rainey, and Cindy Stoeckl

Acknowledgements: Several projects in this book were created with outstanding and innovative products developed by the following manufacturers: Personal Stamp Exchange of Santa Rosa, California, for all rubber stamp supplies and accessories; The Gifted Line, of Point Richmond, California, for permission to use their die cut cards; DMC Corporation, of South Kearny, New Jersey, for floss; Elsie's Exquisites of Lake Forest, California and Quilter's Resource of Chicago, Illinois, for basic ribbon supplies, and specialty trims; and Foss Manufacturing of Hampton, New Hampshire, for Kunin Felt. We would like to offer our sincere appreciation to these companies for the valuable support given in this ever changing industry of new ideas, concepts, designs, and products.

Library of Congress Cataloging-in-Publication Data

Hiney, Mary Jo.
    Making romantic fabric-covered boxes / Mary Jo Hiney.
        p.   cm.
    "A Sterling/Chapelle book."
    Includes index.
    ISBN 0-8069-9995-0
    1. Box craft. 2. Box making. 3. Ornamental boxes. 4. Textile fabrics.
    5. Decoration and ornament—Victorian style. I. Title.
    TT870.5.H493 1998
    745.54—dc21   97—51571
                                                              CIP

10 9 8 7 6 5 4 3 2 1

A Sterling/Chapelle Book

Published by Sterling Publishing Company, Inc.
387 Park Avenue South, New York, NY 10016
© 1998 by Chapelle Ltd.
Distributed in Canada by Sterling Publishing
⅟ Canadian Manda Group, One Atlantic Avenue, Suite 105
Toronto, Ontario, Canada M6K 3E7
Distributed in Great Britain and Europe by Cassell PLC
Wellington House, 125 Strand, London WC2R 0BB, England
Distributed in Australia by Capricorn Link (Australia) Pty Ltd.
P.O. Box 6651, Baulkham Hills, Business Centre, NSW 2153, Australia
Printed and bound in the United States of America
All Rights Reserved

Sterling ISBN 0-8069-9995-0

Due to limited amount of space available, we must print our patterns at a reduced size in order to give our patrons the maximum number of projects possible in our publications. We believe the quality and quantity of our patterns will compensate for any inconvenience this may cause.

The written instructions, photographs, designs, patterns, and projects in this volume are intended for the personal use of the reader and may be reproduced for that purpose only. Any other use, especially commercial use, is forbidden under law without the written permission of the copyright holder.

Every effort has been made to ensure that all of the information in this book is accurate. However, due to differing conditions, tools, and individual skills, the publisher cannot be responsible for any injuries, losses, and/or other damages which may result from the use of the information in this book.

If you have any questions or comments or would like information about any specialty products featured in this book, please contact:

Chapelle Ltd., Inc.
P.O. Box 9252
Ogden, UT 84409

Phone: (801) 621-2777
FAX: (801) 621-2788

CONTENTS

Box Making Basics
6

Box Making Basics

Before making a box, read both the Box Making Basics and the individual box instructions thoroughly and carefully.

Gather the materials and tools you need. Basic tools are listed under "Tools & Materials." Additional tools and materials are listed with the instructions for each box.

Cut all fabric and cardboard. A chart for each box lists how many pieces of fabric and cardboard you need for each pattern piece. When the chart instructs you to add a certain amount to the pattern (e.g., + ¼"), add amount to all sides of pattern.

Many patterns need to be enlarged on a photocopy machine. Patterns that give measurements (e.g., box sides) are best drawn by hand using a precise ruler.

Tools & Materials

Tools

For every box you make you need:

Awl
3"-wide paint roller
Tacky glue
Thin bodied tacky glue
Hot glue gun and glue sticks
Craft scissors
Fabric scissors
Dowels
Heavy and/or lightweight cardboard
Precise ruler
Utility knife
Pencil
Wet and dry rags
Brown paper bag

Paint Roller

Refer to Photo 1. A 3"-wide disposable paint roller spreads glue onto cardboard surfaces just like a paint roller spreads paint onto a wall. It is a wonderful way to achieve thorough coverage of cardboard surfaces. The roller can be washed out with soap and water and reused for many projects. A paint roller may be purchased at a hardware store.

Tacky Glue

Refer to Photo 1. In order to laminate fabric to cardboard, use thin-bodied tacky glue. It bonds fabric to cardboard without staining the fabric. It is the perfect consistency to paint onto cardboard, using a disposable paint roller. The laminating process is half the work and three times the bond when you use the right kind of tacky glue.

Hot Glue Gun & Glue Sticks

Refer to Photo 1. Hot glue is the best glue for box construction. Use the "cloudy" glue stick. The clear sticks do not penetrate fabric well for a good bond, and the yellow sticks are for surfaces like wood. Whenever hot glue is used, it must be flattened thoroughly so bulk is eliminated. (Tacky glue can be used for box construction and all assembly steps, but it needs to be set up for each step and held together with clothespins or masking tape until dry.) You will have the best results using a glue you are most comfortable with.

Embellishment Glues

Refer to Photo 1. Trims can be applied to boxes with hot glue, but tacky glue is the best for gluing trims in place. It is also less tricky than hot glue, but it has to set up a minute or two first. Tacky glue can also bond brass, buttons, and other similar surfaces to the fabric. However, for a better, and more permanent, bond for such items, use an industrial-strength adhesive.

Photo 1

Craft Scissors

Refer to Photo 2. Good craft scissors are essential in order to cut cardboard shapes accurately. Designate a pair of high-quality scissors for cardboard cutting. If you are in the market for a new pair of fabric scissors, retire the old scissors to the position of cardboard cutting. They have a very refined cutting edge, which makes it possible to get into tight areas, and they are very strong. If you are having difficulty cutting cardboard, the thickness of the blades could be the problem.

Fabric Scissors

Refer to Photo 2. Designate a special pair of scissors for cutting fabrics. Using your fabric scissors to cut other materials will dull the blades and make them less effective at cutting fabric.

Dowels

Refer to Photo 2. Wooden dowels are used to shape box sides by rolling. Dowels 8" long and 1", ½", and ¼" wide are enough to get any job done. Substitute a glue stick for ½" dowel and a pencil for a ¼" dowel.

Heavy Cardboard

Refer to Photo 3. You can use crescent board, mat board, or process board. Heavy cardboard is ¹⁄₁₆" thick and sturdy, yet thin enough to be cut with scissors. It can be found at hobby stores and art supply stores. The board should be white on both sides. In most cases, one sheet can make many boxes. Process board is the best, but ¹⁄₁₆"-thick chip board can be used if no other is available.

Photo 2

Lightweight Cardboard

Refer to Photo 3. You can use railroad board, poster board, or chip board. The thinness of these boards makes the cardboard pliable. Railroad and poster board can be white on both sides, whereas chip board is grey. White board is preferred, as the grey board can discolor fabric.

Many stores order railroad board as their poster board. Railroad board has a dull finish; poster board has a shiny finish. It is best to use 6- or 8-ply railroad or poster board. Inquire at the store as to what ply has been ordered. In most cases, one half sheet can make many boxes. If only 4-ply is available, glue two layers together and work them as one.

Precise Ruler

Refer to Photo 3. A metal ruler with precise measurements is essential for making perfect boxes. Yard-sticks and cloth tape measures are not precise!

Utility Knife

Refer to Photo 3. Use a utility knife to score the cardboard. It can also be used to cut some of the more difficult shapes if desired. Use caution and develop skill with this tool. Remember, a sharp blade is safer than a dull blade.

Photo 3

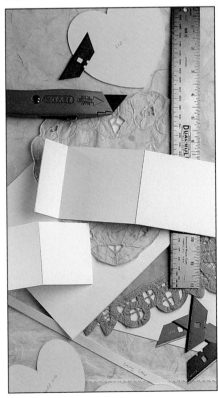

Pencil

Refer to Photo 4. Always keep your pencil as sharp as possible. When measuring, mark cardboard for box sides and scores with a dot at the precise mark to keep measurements accurate.

Rags

A wet rag and a dry rag are necessary to keep hands clean so fabric is not stained with glue.

Brown Paper Bag

An opened brown paper bag is perfect as a "drop cloth." Place cardboard parts onto paper while rolling with glue.

Techniques

Some of the boxes in this book have portions of general assembly in their construction, but in most respects are exceptions to the rules, such as the Cube Boxes, Love Letters, China Hutch, and Cottage Boxes.

Labeling

Label each piece of cardboard in a noticeable but not interfering location, like the center underside. Label each piece of fabric with a piece of pinned paper. Label each piece immediately after cutting. Always keep fabrics and corresponding cardboard pieces together.

Scoring

Refer to Photo 5. Place precision ruler onto score marks. Slice halfway through cardboard with utility knife at marks across width of cardboard. These are mountain scores.

Photo 4

Photo 5

Valley scores are made on the opposite side of the cardboard. Mark location of score at top edge of cardboard side. Flip cardboard over and score. Score cardboard before covering with fabric.

Plain or Fancy

Refer to Photo 6. Any fancy box can be made plain with little or no trims, and any plain box can be made fancy. Trims may be changed on any box. Be creative!

Photo 6

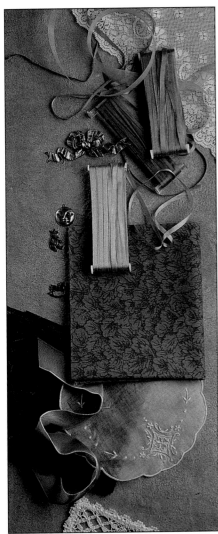

Most silks and lightweight polyesters will stain. Test by laminating onto cardboard scrap if there are any doubts.

The fabric covering process sets the stage for a better finished product. Be precise. At pointed parts of a shape, dab frays with extra glue and wrap frays onto wrong side of cardboard. At indented curves, use fingernail and extra dab of glue to further emphasize shape.

Laminating

When working with silks or polyester fabrics, use <u>Wrapping</u> technique instead of laminating.

Photo 7

Prepare a wet rag and a dry rag for constant hand cleaning. Place or tape brown paper bag onto work surface. Pour enough tacky glue into a disposable plastic or tin dish to cover bottom of dish. Place cardboard onto paper bag. Place fabric wrong side up on work surface.

Refer to Photo 7. Roll glue onto paint roller in dish. Completely cover roller's surface, then roll off extra glue in dish. Paint entire surface of cardboard with glue. Make certain to follow any instructions regarding which side should be laminated if the cardboard is scored.

Surprise Fabric

The first thing anybody does when holding any kind of box is to look inside. Don't disappoint the beholder–choose an inside fabric that is a wonderful surprise!

Fabric-covering Tips

Boxes with inward curves or box insides that are covered with fabric must be laminated. A fabric that will not stain must be used.

Refer to Photo 8. Place glued cardboard on fabric by flipping cardboard over onto wrong side of fabric and pressing in place.

Flip fabric and cardboard over and smooth fabric completely. Eliminate any wrinkles immediately. Pay special attention to edges. Fabric should adhere to cardboard everywhere, especially at the edges.

Refer to Photo 9. Turn laminated cardboard over again. Use roller to paint edges of cardboard and fabric with glue.

Refer to Photo 10. Trim out bulk from each corner, then wrap extended fabric over onto glued edges.

Always double-check corners for fraying fabric, and dab frays with glue and wrap as necessary. Let dry for 10 minutes.

Most BOX SIDES will have one unwrapped edge to be used as a tab to join the BOX SIDES together. Some BOX SIDES are finished on all edges. Make certain to check specific box project instructions for this step.

When laminating BASES, MIDDLE LIDS, LIDS, etc., make certain to trim bulk from corners and clip fabric at all inward curves as precisely wrapped parts are essential. Unless otherwise specified, wrap fabric around all edges of shaped piece.

Wrapping

Refer to Photo 11. Place fabric onto work surface, right side down. Center cardboard over fabric. Make certain to follow any instructions regarding which side should be wrapped if the cardboard is scored. Trim out bulk from any corners, then snugly and squarely wrap and glue edges of fabric over cardboard.

Double-check corners for fraying fabric, and dab frays with glue if necessary. Let dry for 10 minutes.

Padding & Wrapping

Refer to Photo 12. Lightly glue surface of cardboard shape. Place onto batting.

Refer to Photo 13. Trim batting flush to cardboard's edge, beveling scissors inward slightly.

Refer to Photo 14. Place fabric wrong side up on work surface. Center padded cardboard over fabric.

Glue 1" at inner edge of cardboard. Snugly and squarely wrap fabric onto glue. On opposite edge, glue and wrap another 1" worth of fabric onto cardboard. Trim all bulk from corners and clip curves as necessary.

Continue to glue and wrap fabric onto cardboard a small amount at a time, pulling the fabric as snugly as possible. Exact shape of cardboard should not be altered when fabric is wrapped.

Photo 8

Photo 9

Photo 10

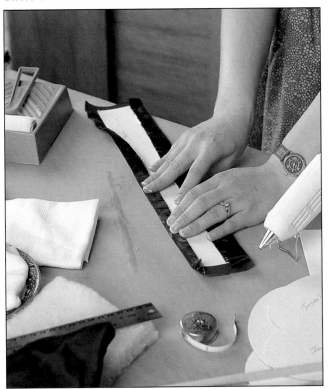

Photo 11

Photo 12

Photo 13

Photo 14

Rolling Cardboard with Dowel

Score lines are always emphasized after cardboard is covered and before cardboard is rolled. Refer to Diagram 1. Fold cardboard at score and roll 1" dowel over fold.

Some boxes have both mountain scores and valley scores. Make certain to fold scores on appropriate side.

Refer to Photo 15. Place cardboard on work surface, required side up. Place dowel at outer edge of cardboard. Begin to wrap cardboard around dowel without squaring off cardboard.

Continue to roll remaining length of cardboard as indicated in box directions. Use inside bottom shape as a guide to mold cardboard.

For detailed shaping, some boxes will require a ¼" dowel and finger molding.

Diagram 1

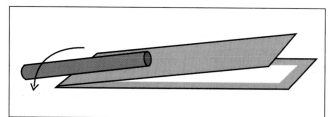

Photo 15

Box Construction

Assembling Style A Box Side & Bottom

Refer to Photo 16. Join short edges of BOX SIDE by overlapping tab fabric edge to finished short edge and butting edges up to each other. Glue tab in place.

Refer to Diagram 2. Working upside down, slip INSIDE BOTTOM or compartments into box ¹⁄₁₆" down from edge of BOX SIDE.

Using a thin bead of hot glue, attach INSIDE BOTTOM to box. Glue 1" at a time and hold until glue dries, then proceed.

Re-emphasize shape of box by molding with fingers.

Photo 16

Diagram 2

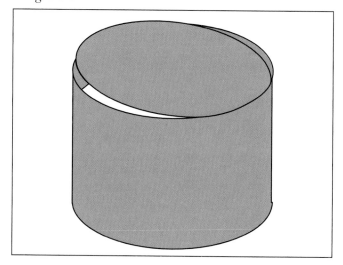

Assembling Style B Box Side & Bottom

Refer to Photo 17. Snugly wrap BOX SIDE around INSIDE BOTTOM. Hold in place and mark overlap.

Overlap and glue one short edge of BOX SIDE to opposite edge at mark.

Complete bottom assembly in same manner as Style A.

Photo 17

Gluing Ribbon/Fabric Hinge
to inside of Box Side

If a hinge is required for the lid, insert it at this point. Glue ribbon/ fabric hinge(s) onto inside of BOX SIDE at overlap.

Lining Boxes

Section INSIDE BOTTOM LINING into quarters and notch. Section LINING STRIP into quarters and mark.

Refer to Photo 18. With right side up, match notches of INSIDE BOTTOM LINING to LINING STRIP and glue. Refer to Photo 19. Finger-gather or gather-stitch lining fabric between notches to fit LINING STRIP.

Photo 18

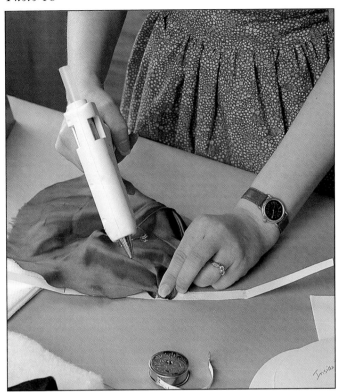

Photo 19

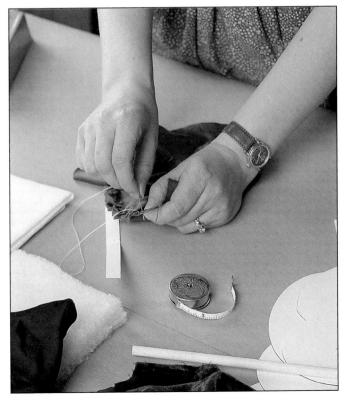

13

Refer to Photo 20. Glue gathered fabric to strip. When all fabric has been glued to strip, the strip becomes circular and inside out. Turn lining right side out. Fold cardboard strip down, so that lining has finished edge. Place quilt batting inside box.

Refer to Photos 21, 22, and 23. Beginning at center of strip and center front of box, glue lining strip to top inside edge of box, making certain to keep any hinges extended out from box. Thoroughly flatten glue.

Photo 22

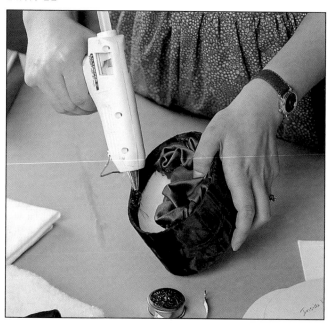

Photo 20

Photo 23

Photo 21

Gluing Ribbon/Fabric Hinge
to Inside Lid

Refer to Photo 24. Rest INSIDE LID, right side down, into top edge of the box, and hold in place. Glue ribbon/fabric hinge(s) onto wrong side of INSIDE LID, creating a snug fit.

Center and glue wrong side of INSIDE LID to

14

right side of MIDDLE LID. Flatten glue thoroughly.

Photo 24

Photo 25

Laminating Lid Strip

Place lid strip fabric wrong side up on work surface. Paint LID STRIP with laminating glue. Make certain to follow any instructions regarding which side should be down if the cardboard is scored. Refer to Photo 25. Place glued LID STRIP ¼" up from one long edge of fabric and centered between short edges. Flip fabric and cardboard over. Completely smooth fabric to cardboard. Make certain fabric is entirely adhered to all edges of cardboard. Refer to Photo 26. Trim off the ¼" excess fabric from bottom edge of cardboard. Fabric covered side is the inside of the LID STRIP.

Refer to Photo 27. Place LID STRIP on work surface, uncovered side up. Glue ½" of one short edge of fabric. Wrap short edge over on itself at cardboard's edge. Do not glue or cut opposite short edge of fabric as it will be used as a tab to join the edges together. For LID STRIPS that overlap when assembling lid, follow instructions given for the individual box.

The LID STRIP is now completely covered with fabric and ½" of fabric extends past cardboard's long edge.

Extended fabric side of cardboard is the outside of the lid strip. Let dry for 10 minutes and then roll, if necessary.

Photo 26

Photo 27

Assembling Lid

For a tab edge LID STRIP, join short edges by overlapping tab edge onto finished edge and adjoining cardboard edges to each other. Glue tab in place on outside of LID STRIP.

For LID STRIPS that overlap, snugly wrap LID STRIP around INSIDE LID. Hold in place and mark overlap, with finished edge inside. Overlap and glue finished short edge of LID STRIP to opposite edge of at mark.

Refer to Photo 28. Slip INSIDE LID into LID STRIP at trimmed edge. Working upside down, glue edge of INSIDE LID to trimmed edge of LID STRIP, working small sections at a time. Fold extending fabric from LID STRIP down over outside of LID STRIP. If desired, fabric can be laminated to outside of LID STRIP at this time.

Refer to Photo 29. Glue extended fabric over onto wrong side of INSIDE LID, pulling fabric tight for a snug fit.

Continue to glue extended fabric of LID STRIP completely onto shape. Clip curves as necessary and thoroughly flatten glue.

Photo 28

Photo 29

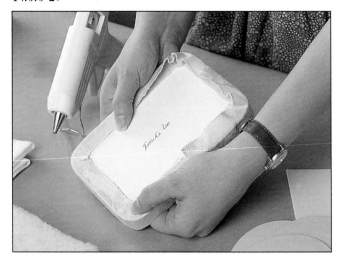

Cross-stitch

Cross-stitch

Stitches are done in a row or, if necessary, one at a time in an area. Stitching is done by coming up through a hole between woven threads at A. Then, go down at B, the hole diagonally across from A. Come back up at C and down at D, etc. Complete the top stitches to create an "X". All top stitches should lie in the same direction. Come up at E and go down at B, come up at C and go down at F, etc.

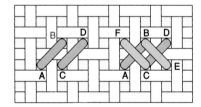

Backstitch

Pull the needle through at the point marked A. Then go down one opening to the right, at B. Then, come back up at C. Now, go down one opening to the right, this time at "A".

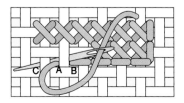

French Knot

(1) Bring needle up at A, using two strands of embroidery floss. Loosely wrap floss once around needle.

(2) Place needle at B, next to A. Pull floss taut as you push needle down through fabric. Carry floss across back of work between knots.

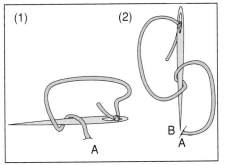

Embroidery Work

Tracing

When tracing transfer diagrams onto fabric, use a disappearing pen. You do not have to transfer all marks—use them as a general placement guide.

Ribbon Tips

Always keep the ribbon loose and flat while working stitches. Untwist ribbon often and pull ribbon softly so it lies flat on top of fabric. Be creative with the stitching. Exact stitch placement is not critical, but make sure any placement marks are covered.

Needles

A size 3 crewel embroidery needle works well for most fabrics when using 4mm ribbon. For 7mm ribbon, use a chenille needle, sizes 18 to 24. As a rule of thumb, the barrel of the needle must create a hole large enough for the ribbon to pass through. If ribbon does not pull through fabric easily, a larger needle is needed.

To Thread Ribbon on Needle

(1) Thread the ribbon through the eye of the needle. With the tip of the needle, pierce the center of the ribbon ¼" from end.

(2) Pull remaining ribbon through to "lock" ribbon on needle.

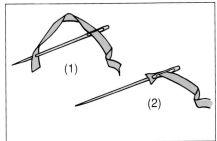

Knotting End of Ribbon

(1) Drape the ribbon in a circular manner to position the end of the ribbon perpendicular to the tip of the needle.

(2) Pierce the end of the ribbon with the needle, sliding the needle through the ribbon as if to make a short basting stitch.

(3) Pull needle and ribbon through the stitch portion to form a knot at end of ribbon.

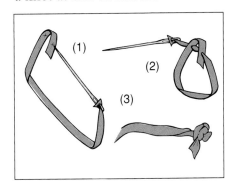

To End Stitching

Secure stitches in place for each flower or small area. Do not drag the ribbon from one area to another. Tie a slip knot on the wrong side of needlework to secure the stitch in place and end ribbon.

Embroidery Stitches

Beading Stitch

Using one strand of floss, come up through fabric. Slide the bead on the needle and push the needle back down through fabric. Knot off each bead or set of beads.

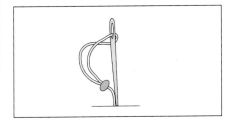

Cascading Stitch

The cascading stitch can be done starting with a bow or just a length of ribbon and cascading "streamers" through design.

When starting with a bow, leave streamers long enough to work cascade through design. Thread streamer on needle, stitch down through fabric where bow placement is desired and come back up at start of cascade effect. This will hold the bow in place.

(1) Come up at A and go down at B. Come back up at C, allowing ribbon to twist and lay loosely on the fabric.

(2) Go down again at B and come up at C, making a small backstitch. This keeps the cascading in place.

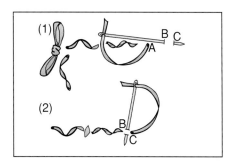

Circular Ruffle

(1) Fold required ribbon in half, matching cut ends. Gather-stitch along one selvage edge. Tightly gather and secure thread.

(2) Completed Circular Ruffle.

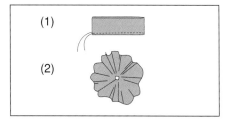

Colonial Knot

(1) Bring needle up through fabric at A. Drape ribbon in a backward "C". Place needle through "C".

(2) Wrap ribbon over needle and under tip of the needle forming a figure-8. Hold knot firmly on needle. Insert needle through fabric close to A. Hold ribbon securely until knot is formed on top of fabric.

(3) Completed Colonial Knot.

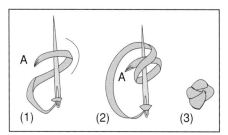

Cross-over Lazy Daisy

(1) Bring needle up at A. Cross over to right of ribbon, and insert needle at B. Come back up at C and pull ribbon to desired shape.

(2) Go down at D making a Straight Stitch to tack loop.

(3) Completed Cross-over Lazy Daisy.

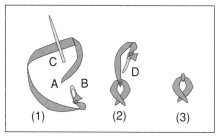

Flute

Fluting is usually used as a trim. Glue one ribbon end to fabric or underside of cardboard. Loop ¼" deep and glue keeping ribbon angled. Repeat, making a series of even, angled loops.

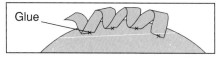

Folded Leaf

(1) Cut ribbon to desired length. Overlap ends of ribbon

(2) Gather-stitch at bottom edge.

(3) Gather tightly. Wrap thread around stitches to secure. Trim excess ⅛" past stitching.

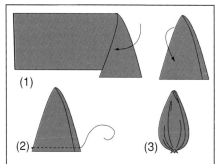

Gathered Rose

(1) Fold 1 short edge at a 90° angle.

(2) Fold bottom corner over at a 90° angle.

(3) Roll folded ribbon and secure. Gather-stitch half of remaining ribbon. Pull thread and wrap gather around folded ribbon.

(4) Gather-stitch remaining ribbon. Wrap gather around.

(5) Completed gathered rose.

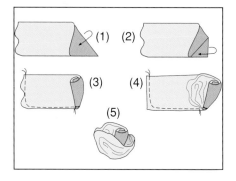

Gathered Rosebud

(1) Fold ribbon

(2) Fold again.

(3) Roll folded end and secure at bottom of roll. Gather-stitch opposite end.

(4) Tightly gather to form petal and secure thread. Wrap gathered petal around center roll to form bud.

(5) Completed Gathered Rosebud.

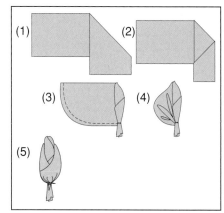

Generous Rose Stitch

(1) Insert two darning needles into fabric, criss crossed.

(2) Knot ribbon and bring to surface at center of criss-crossed needles.

Wind ribbon loosely around needles, beginning by crossing over needles to cover center.

Twist the ribbon one or two times while winding for texture.

Invisibly hand-tack wound ribbon to fabric using matching thread.

(4) Remove criss-crossed needles once ribbon is stationary.

(5) Insert needles again into fabric, placing needles criss-crossed underneath the outermost layer of wound ribbon.

(6) Bring second ribbon shade to surface, hiding entry point.

Loosely wind second ribbon shade around needles 1½ times. Hand-tack as before and remove needles.

(7) Hand gather-stitch 3" to 4" of remaining ribbon along selvage edge. Pull thread to gather ribbon and position around wound ribbon. Stitch into fabric at end of gathers to secure.

Continue to hand gather-stitch short lengths of ribbon, filling out rose until it is the desired size (about 1½ times around outermost layer of wound ribbon). Stitch into ribbon at end of gathering to hide ribbon end. Hand-tack gathered edge of ribbon to fabric.

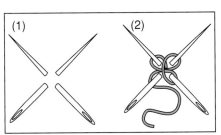

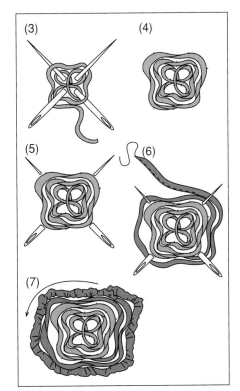

Knotted & Looped Ribbon Stitch

(1) Bring ribbon to surface. Tie a knot in ribbon ¼" from entry point, or the amount indicated in instructions.

(2) Fold ribbon over on itself from knot. Stitch into ribbon and fabric directly next to base of entry point to complete stitch.

(3) Allow entire looped and knotted ribbon to remain above surface for a completed Knotted & Looped Ribbon Stitch.

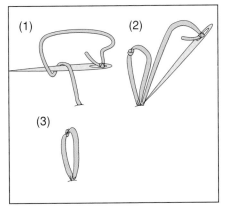

Knotted Petals

(1) Tie a knot at center of each length. Place ribbons in like color piles.

(2) Fold lengths in half with knot at top, matching cut ends. Alternate ribbon shades while chain gather-stitching them together, taking a ½" seam.

(3) When all petals have been chained together, tightly gather and secure thread. Keep knotted ends facing same direction. Join last petal to first. Trim cut ends to ⅛" below stitching. Completed Knotted Petals.

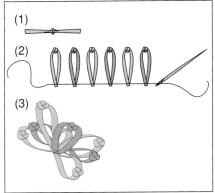

Layered Ribbon Stitch

(1) Refer to Ribbon Stitch. Work Ribbon Stitches to fill area.

(2) Work a second layer of Ribbon Stitches over the first layer.

(3) Completed Layered Ribbon Stitch.

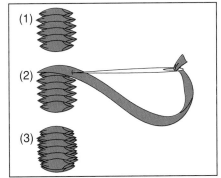

Lazy Daisy

(1) Bring the needle up at A. Keep the ribbon flat, untwisted and full. Put the needle down through fabric at B and up at C, keeping the ribbon under the needle to form a loop. Pull the ribbon through, leaving the loop loose and full. To hold the loop in place, go down on other side of ribbon near C, forming a straight stitch over loop.

(2) Completed lazy daisy.

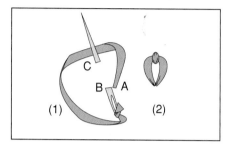

One-twist Ribbon Stitch

(1) Bring needle up at A. Extend ribbon its full length and twist needle once so ribbon coils but not so tight it buckles.

Insert needle back into twisted ribbon at B.

(2) Pull needle through ribbon and fabric, allowing some of the ends of the ribbon to curl.

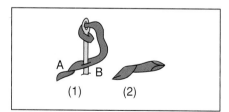

Outline Stitch

Working from left to right, make slightly slanting stitches along the line of the outline. Come up at A, and insert needle through fabric at B keeping thread or ribbon to the right and above the needle. Bring needle up at C (halfway between A and B). Make all stitches the same length. Insert needle through fabric at D (half the length of the stitch beyond B), and continue in the same manner.

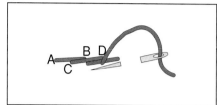

Pointed Petal Stitch

(1) Bring needle up at A. Turn ribbon under at a 45° angle and then forward at a 45° angle to meet entry point.

(2) Stitch needle into ribbon and fabric at B, right next to entry point.

(3) Tack or press ribbon point as desired for a completed Pointed Petal Stitch.

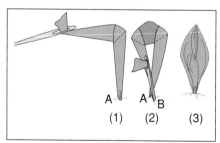

Ribbon Stitch

(1) Come up through fabric at the starting point of stitch. Lay the ribbon flat on the fabric. At the end of the stitch, pierce the ribbon with the needle. Slowly pull the length of the ribbon through to the back, allowing the ends of the ribbon to curl. If the ribbon is pulled too tightly, the effect of the stitch can be lost. Vary the petals and leaves by adjusting the length, the tension of the ribbon before piercing, the position of piercing, and how loosely or tightly the ribbon is pulled down through itself.

(2) Completed Ribbon Stitch.

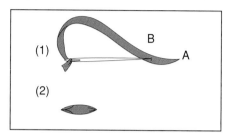

Ribbonwork Daisy

(1) Press and fold each length of ribbon forward to overlap at cut ends. Pin to hold.

(2) Chain gather-stitch all petals together. Tightly pull gather and secure thread. Adjust gather so petals are evenly spaced. Follow project instructions for joining last petal to first petal.

(3) Completed Ribbonwork Daisy.

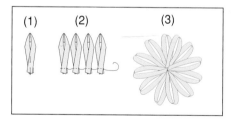

Ribbonwork Grape

(1) Gather-stitch all 4 edges of a square of ribbon, ⅛" from edge.

(2) Pull thread to gather as tightly as possible.

(3) Collapse ribbon, as for a yo-yo.

(4) Gather stitch along outer, folded edge of collapsed ribbon. Pull gathers as tight as possible while stuffing collapsed ribbon inward. Secure thread.

This technique eliminates the need for stuffing, as it is self stuffing, and makes very small grapes, berries or flower centers.

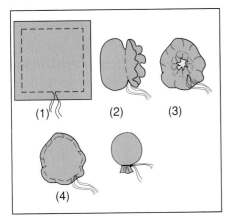

Rosette

(1) Fold length of ribbon down at right angle, creating a post to hold onto.

(2) Fold folded end in half. Stitch in place securely with thread.

(3) Continue rolling and folding ribbon. Stitch to secure.

(4) When ribbon is folded and rolled half its length, hand-stitch a gathering stitch along the bottom edge of remaining length of ribbon. Tightly pull gathering stitch and wrap gathered section around folded rose. Stitch in place to secure.

(5) Completed Rosette.

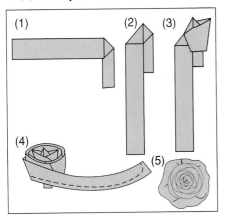

Ruffled Ribbon Stitch with Hand-gathered Sections

(1) Bring ribbon to surface. Mark 2" from entry point, or the amount indicated in instructions.

Thread hand-sewing needle with matching, doubled thread. Bring thread to surface at ribbon entry point. Gather-stitch along selvage edge of ribbon to mark.

(2) Pull gathers for desired stitch length. Insert hand-sewing needle back into fabric, securing thread and gathers.

(3) To complete, stitch ribbon needle into ribbon and through fabric in same manner as a Ribbon Stitch.

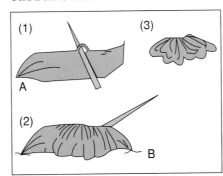

Squared Petal

(1) The interval of the gathering stitches must be greater than the width of the ribbon to make a Squared Petal.

(2) Pull thread to gather and secure. Shape petal as desired.

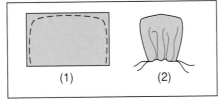

Zinnia

(1) Cut ribbon into required number of petals, using pattern provided (enlarge 200%).

(2) Alternate pattern onto ribbon when cutting petals to eliminate waste and utilize both ribbon shades.

(3) Chain gather-stitch all petals together. Tightly gather stitches and secure thread.

(4) Join last petal to first petal. Shape petals and pinch tips. Stitch to hold in place.

(5) Completed Zinnia.

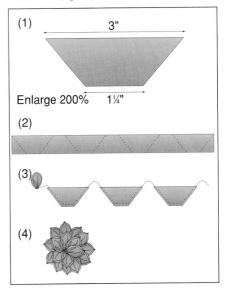

Stamping & Embossing

Embossing powders are available in many opaque colors, as well as metallic, iridescent, and sparklers, which contain glitter.

Heat tools are made for embossing. They get very hot, but they do not blow much air.

Stamp an image on a slow-drying pigment pad. Apply the image to paper surface. Pour embossing powder on image. Tap off excess embossing powder. Heat with a heat tool until powder melts. Re-ink after each impression and repeat the embossing process.

serene,
Their
dresses
tied
with
sashes,
and
futures
tied
with
dreams...

1 An Offering

Fairy Tokens

Heavy Cardboard	Light Cardboard
BASE and MIDDLE LID (Cut 2)	BOX SIDE
LID	
INSIDE BOTTOM	
INSIDE LID (Cut 4)	

Three Coordinating Shades of Paper:		
from one paper	from second paper	from third paper
BOX SIDE: 2½" x 28½"	inside of BOX SIDE: 2" x 27¼"	bottom strip on outside
MIDDLE LID + ¾"	MIDDLE LID: tear to fit	of BOX SIDE: 1½" x 27¼"
	finished size	BASE + ¾"
		INSIDE LID + ¾"

Cotton Fabric	Quilt Batting
LID + 1"	INSIDE BOTTOM
	LID

Tools & Materials

Heavy cardboard: 32" x 20"
Light cardboard: 27¼" x 1½"
Cotton fabric: 12" x 8" (peach broadcloth)
Papers: three sheets of 36" x 8" (lt. green, olive green, and lavender Japanese mulberry)
Quilt batting: 9" x 22"

Trim: ⅞ yd. of 1"-wide (ecru lace)
Silk ribbons: ½ yd. of 4mm (dk. yellow); 3 yds. of 7mm (mint green ombré); 1 yd. of 13mm (ivory), 1 yd. of 13mm (mint green ombré); 1 yd. of 13mm (olive green); 1 yd. of 13mm (peach ombré); 1½ yds. of 13mm (dk. pink); 1½ yds. of 13mm (lt. pink ombré)

Sheer ribbon: 1½ yds. of 24mm (ivory)
Rhinestones: two ⅛" (crystal), one ¼" (mauve) butterflies
Acrylic paints: aqua, bronze, brown, crimson, flesh, mint green, olive green, iridescent gold, lavender, peach, violet, white
Textile medium

Industrial-strength adhesive
Needles: size 20 chenille; large-eyed darning; hand-sewing
Paintbrush: liner
Paint palette: washable
Cotton swabs
Thread: coordinating

Directions

1. Cut Cardboard and Fabric; Score

2. Following Fairy Tokens Painting Guide and Diagram on pages 24 and 25, trace pattern onto right side of LID fabric for paint guide. Blend acrylic paints on palette to achieve desired shades and thin with textile medium and a small amount of water. Paint fairy using a cotton swab for each paint shade and to blend paints into each other for a watercolor effect. Allow painted fairy to dry completely.

Description	Paint Shade	Technique
1. Face	flesh	Blend skin shades, fill face.
2. Pupils, Eyebrows, Outline facial features	brown	Paint pupils. Use thin strokes for eyebrows and to outline eyes, nose, mouth, chin, and lips.
3. Eyes	White	Paint irises and place dot in right pupil corner.
4. Hair	brown, bronze	Swirl brown and bronze shades for hair.
5. Wings	aqua, lavender, peach, violet	Use all shades for wings. Place peach at outer wing edges.
6. Outline Wings	olive green	Use a thin stroke to outline shape of wings.
7. Gown	mint green, peach	Blend shades at gown area.
8. Overall	iridescent gold	Cover entire flower fairy with a thin coat of iridescent gold.

3. Enlarge Fairy Tokens Transfer Diagram on opposite page and transfer to painted fabric. Embroider fabric following Fairy Tokens Stitch Guide below and on opposite page.

Description	Ribbon	Stitch
1. Petals	pink	Ruffled Ribbon Stitch with hand-gathered sections
2. Petals	peach	Ruffled Ribbon Stitch with hand-gathered sections
3. Petals	dk. pink	Pointed Petal Stitch
4. Petals	ivory	Ruffled Ribbon Stitch with hand-gathered sections
5. Largest Petals	sheer	Pointed Petal Stitch
6. Stamens	dk. yellow	Knotted and Looped Ribbon Stitch
7. Leaves	olive green	1-Twist Ribbon Stitch
8. Leaves	ivory	1-Twist Ribbon Stitch
9. Leaves	13mm mint green ombré	1-Twist Ribbon Stitch
10. Bow	7mm mint green ombré (18" length)	Cascading Stitch

4. Cover Cardboard with Fabric and Paper; Shape

Refer to Box Making Basics for Laminating on page 9. Working quickly, laminate mountain-scored side of BOX SIDE with light green paper. Finish all four edges. Tear one long edge of lavender paper. Laminate over light green paper, placing torn edge about ¾" down from top edge. Tear one long edge of olive green paper. Laminate to valley-scored side of BOX SIDE, placing torn edge near top inside edge. Trim bottom edge flush to cardboard. Immediately fold BOX SIDE on score lines. Place valley-scored side up on work surface and roll entire BOX SIDE with a 1"

Fairy Tokens Painting Diagram

Fairy Tokens Transfer Diagram   Enlarge 230%

Fairy Tokens Stitch Guide

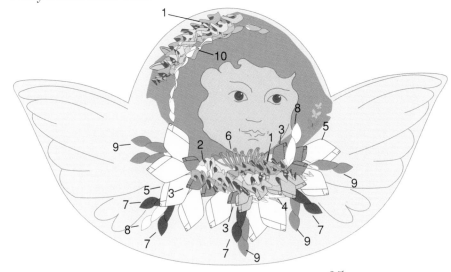

She said she would give him a kiss if he liked, but Peter did not know what she meant, and he held out his hand expectantly. "Surely you know what a kiss is?" she asked. "I shall know when you give it to me," he replied; and not to hurt his feeling she gave him a thimble.

—from Peter Pan by J.M. Barrie

dowel. Beginning at mountain scores, roll BOX SIDE in opposite direction, inward to center, for 3".

Laminate MIDDLE LID with light green paper. Tear edges from olive green paper and laminate to underside of MIDDLE LID.

Glue four INSIDE LIDS together as one. Laminate INSIDE LID with lavender paper.

Laminate BASE with lavender paper.

Refer to Box Making Basics for Padding and Wrapping on page 10 and pad INSIDE BOTTOM with quilt batting, then wrap with olive green mulberry paper. Clip paper as needed at curves and corners.

Pad LID with quilt batting, then center and wrap with embroidered flower fairy. Clip at curves and corners as needed. Sew small straight stitches around hair line on face and on nose, mouth, and chin to accentuate facial features. Glue rhinestone butterflies to hair using industrial-strength adhesive.

5. Assemble Box Bottom; Embellish

Beginning at an inside wing corner and working small sections at a time, glue edge of INSIDE BOTTOM to bottom edge of BOX SIDE. Overlap short ends at center top of head curve. Redefine box shape by molding with fingers.

Laminate trim to top edge of BOX SIDE. Flute while gluing 7mm mint green ribbon to underside edge on bottom of box.

Glue wrong side of BASE to bottom of box. Center and glue wrong side of INSIDE LID to olive green side of MIDDLE LID. Glue wrong side of LID to MIDDLE LID.

Fairy Tokens Patterns

Fairy Tokens Patterns   Enlarge 200%

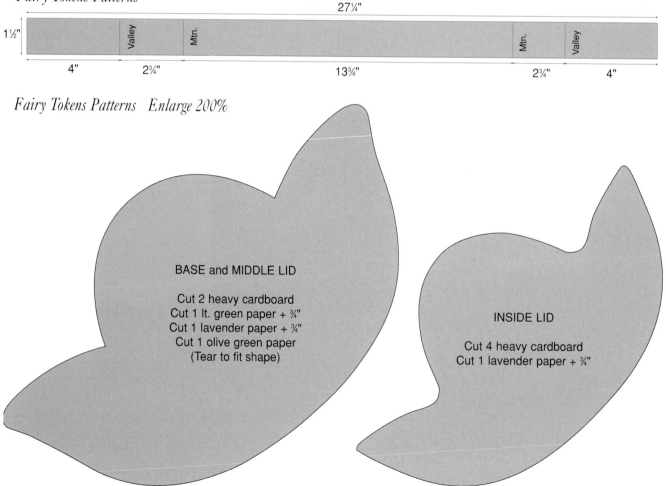

BASE and MIDDLE LID

Cut 2 heavy cardboard
Cut 1 lt. green paper + ¾"
Cut 1 lavender paper + ¾"
Cut 1 olive green paper
(Tear to fit shape)

INSIDE LID

Cut 4 heavy cardboard
Cut 1 lavender paper + ¾"

Fairy Tokens Patterns   Enlarge 200%

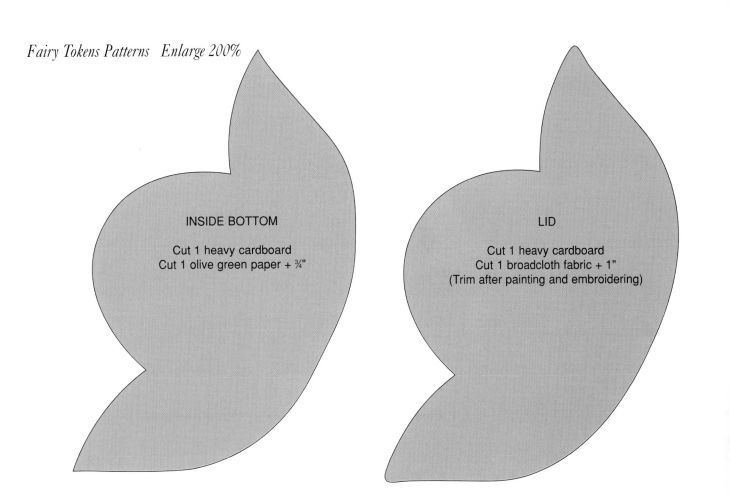

INSIDE BOTTOM

Cut 1 heavy cardboard
Cut 1 olive green paper + ¾"

LID

Cut 1 heavy cardboard
Cut 1 broadcloth fabric + 1"
(Trim after painting and embroidering)

Poppies & Roses

Heavy Cardboard	Light Cardboard
LID	OUTSIDE BOX SIDE
INSIDE LID, INSIDE BOTTOM, and TRAY LINER (Cut 3)	INSIDE BOX SIDE
	TRAY SIDE
BASE	DIVIDED TRAY
	HIDDEN LID STRIP

Outside Fabric	Coordinating Outside Fabric	Inside Fabric
LID + ¾"	2½" x 22½" decorative strip for bottom of OUTSIDE BOX SIDE	INSIDE BOX SIDE + ¾"
OUTSIDE BOX SIDE: 22½" x 7½", + 2" x 7½" strip	BASE + ¾"	TRAY SIDE: 3½" x 22"
		HIDDEN LID STRIP: 2½" x 22"
		DIVIDED TRAY + ¾"
		INSIDE LID + ¾"
		INSIDE BOTTOM + ¾"
		TRAY LINER + ¾"

Hat Veiling	Quilt Batting
LID + ¾"	LID
	INSIDE BOX SIDE
	INSIDE BOTTOM

Tools & Materials

Heavy cardboard: 8" x 30"

Light cardboard: 15" x 34"

Outside fabric: ¼ yd. of 44"-wide (muted coral print)

Coordinating outside fabric: ¼ yd. of 44"-wide (small coral print)

Inside fabric: ½ yd. of 44"-wide (red/coral print)

Quilt batting: 30" x 6"

Hat veiling: 8½" x 6½" (brown)

Trims: 24" of ¹⁄₁₆"-wide (burgundy picot); 1 yd. of ⅝"-wide (ecru lace); 12" of 1"-wide (ecru lace); 20" of 1¼"-wide (ecru lace)

Chenille: 30" of ⅛"-wide (coral)

Bias-cut ribbon: 12" of 2½"-wide (olive green)

Wire-edge ribbon: 6" of ⅞"-wide (olive green ombré)

Silk ribbon: 18" of 7mm (dk. red)

Velvet leaves: three 2"

Beads: 160 seed (shades of coral)

Fabric dye (taupe)

Beading wire

Needle: hand-sewing

Wire cutters

Directions

1. Cut Cardboard and Fabric; Score

2. Cover Cardboard with Fabric; Mark; Shape

Refer to Box Making Basics for <u>Laminating</u> on page 9 and laminate OUTSIDE BOX SIDE with outside fabric. Center and place cardboard on fabric between short ends and ¾" up from one long edge. This will be bottom edge. Trim fabric. Finish bottom edge and sides. Trim excess fabric from top corners of short ends of extended fabric edge then wrap extended fabric to inside of OUTSIDE BOX SIDE.

Invisibly mark wrong side of OUTSIDE BOX SIDE where indicated on pattern. Place OUTSIDE BOX SIDE inside up on work surface and roll cardboard at marks with a 1" dowel to create rounded corners. Mold with finger to add shape.

Laminate HIDDEN LID STRIP and TRAY SIDE with inside fabric. Follow instructions for <u>Laminating Lid Strip</u> on page 15. Invisibly mark inside of HIDDEN LID STRIP and TRAY SIDE where indicated on pattern. Place each inside up on work surface and roll in same manner as OUTSIDE BOX SIDE.

Laminate BASE with coordinating outside fabric. Laminate INSIDE LID, TRAY LINER, and mountain scored side of DIVIDED TRAY with inside fabric. Fold DIVIDED TRAY on score lines when dry.

Refer to General Instructions for <u>Padding and Wrapping</u> on page 11 and pad INSIDE BOX SIDE with quilt batting, then wrap long edges and one short end with inside fabric. Mark underside of INSIDE BOX SIDE where indicated on pattern. Roll in same manner as OUTSIDE BOX SIDE with fabric right side up. Pad INSIDE BOTTOM with quilt batting, then wrap with inside fabric.

Pad LID with quilt batting, then wrap with outside fabric. Overlay and wrap hat veiling around LID.

3. Assemble Box Bottom

Overlap tab fabric onto underside of finished short edge of INSIDE BOX SIDE, adjoining short cardboard edge, and glue tab in place. Working upside-down, glue edge of INSIDE BOTTOM to one long edge of INSIDE BOX SIDE. Place seam of INSIDE BOX SIDE at center of one long edge of INSIDE

BOTTOM. Match rounded corners of INSIDE BOX SIDE to rounded corners of INSIDE BOTTOM. Continue to glue INSIDE BOX SIDE to INSIDE BOX BOTTOM until complete. Redefine box shape at corners.

Glue right side of short edge of 2" x 7½" outside fabric strip to underside top edge of INSIDE BOX SIDE at joint.

Wrap and glue OUTSIDE BOX SIDE to INSIDE BOX SIDE, wrong sides together, matching rounded corners and adjoining short ends. Laminate 2"-wide strip over adjoined ends of OUT-SIDE BOX SIDE, from inside to outside.

Laminate 2"-wide coordinating outside fabric strip to bottom edge of OUTSIDE BOX SIDE, extending fabric ¾" past bottom edge. Glue extended fabric onto box bottom.

Glue wrong side of BASE to bottom of box.

4. Assemble Divided Tray and Lid

Glue wrong side of DIVIDED TRAY together in-between valley scores, creating two stand-up dividers.

Refer to Box Making Basics for <u>Assembling Lid</u> on page 16 and assemble TRAY SIDE to DIVIDED TRAY. Begin at center of one long edge of DIVIDED TRAY. Attach HIDDEN LID STRIP to INSIDE LID in same manner.

Glue wrong side of TRAY LINER to underside of DIVIDED TRAY.

5. Embellish Box

Dye lace trims in fabric dye

following manufacturer's instructions. Remove lace from dye bath when lace trims are two shades darker than desired.

Laminate and glue ⅝"-wide lace trim to top edge of coordinating outside fabric strip on OUTSIDE BOX SIDE.

Referring to photograph on page 28 for placement, glue 1¼"-wide lace trim across one corner of LID. Cover straight edge of lace trim with ⅝"-wide lace trim.

Glue picot trim to bottom of box in-between gully at BASE and OUTSIDE BOX SIDE.

Cut 1¼"-wide lace trim into three 5" lengths and make three <u>Gathered Rosebuds</u>. Glue in place.

Make a <u>Squared Petal</u> using 1"-wide lace trim. Glue in place.

Fold bias ribbon in half, matching long edges. Press. Make three <u>Folded Leaves</u>. Glue in place.

Make two <u>Folded Leaves</u> using wire-edge ribbon. Glue in place.

Tuck and glue velvet leaves in place.

Fold chenille into a cluster of eight loops that are each ¾" deep. Stitch or wire loops together at one edge. Repeat for a second cluster. Glue chenille loop clusters in place.

Slip 20 seed beads onto a 4" length of beading wire. Fold wire in half and twist ends together to form a beaded loop. Repeat, making eight beaded loops and alternating bead shades. Twist all loops together and glue in place.

Fold silk ribbon in half and tie into a small bow near center of ribbon. Glue ribbon in place.

Poppies & Roses Patterns   Enlarge 230%

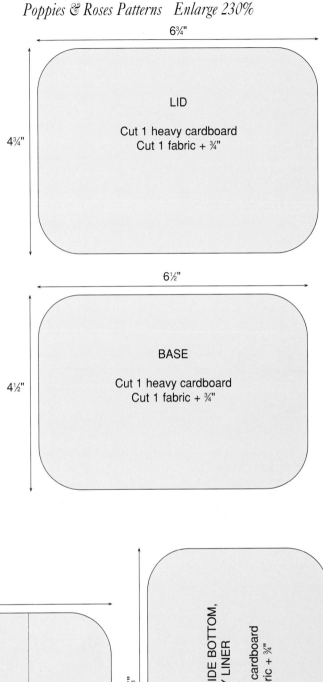

6¾"

4¾"

LID

Cut 1 heavy cardboard
Cut 1 fabric + ¾"

6½"

4½"

BASE

Cut 1 heavy cardboard
Cut 1 fabric + ¾"

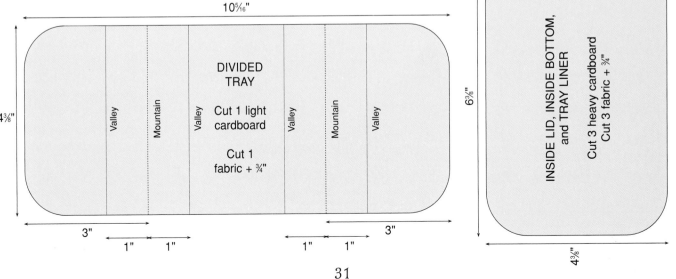

10⁵⁄₁₆"

4⅜"

DIVIDED TRAY

Cut 1 light cardboard

Cut 1 fabric + ¾"

Valley Mountain Valley Valley Mountain Valley

3"

1" 1"

3"

1" 1"

INSIDE LID, INSIDE BOTTOM, and TRAY LINER

Cut 3 heavy cardboard
Cut 3 fabric + ¾"

6⅜"

4⅜"

Poppies & Roses Patterns

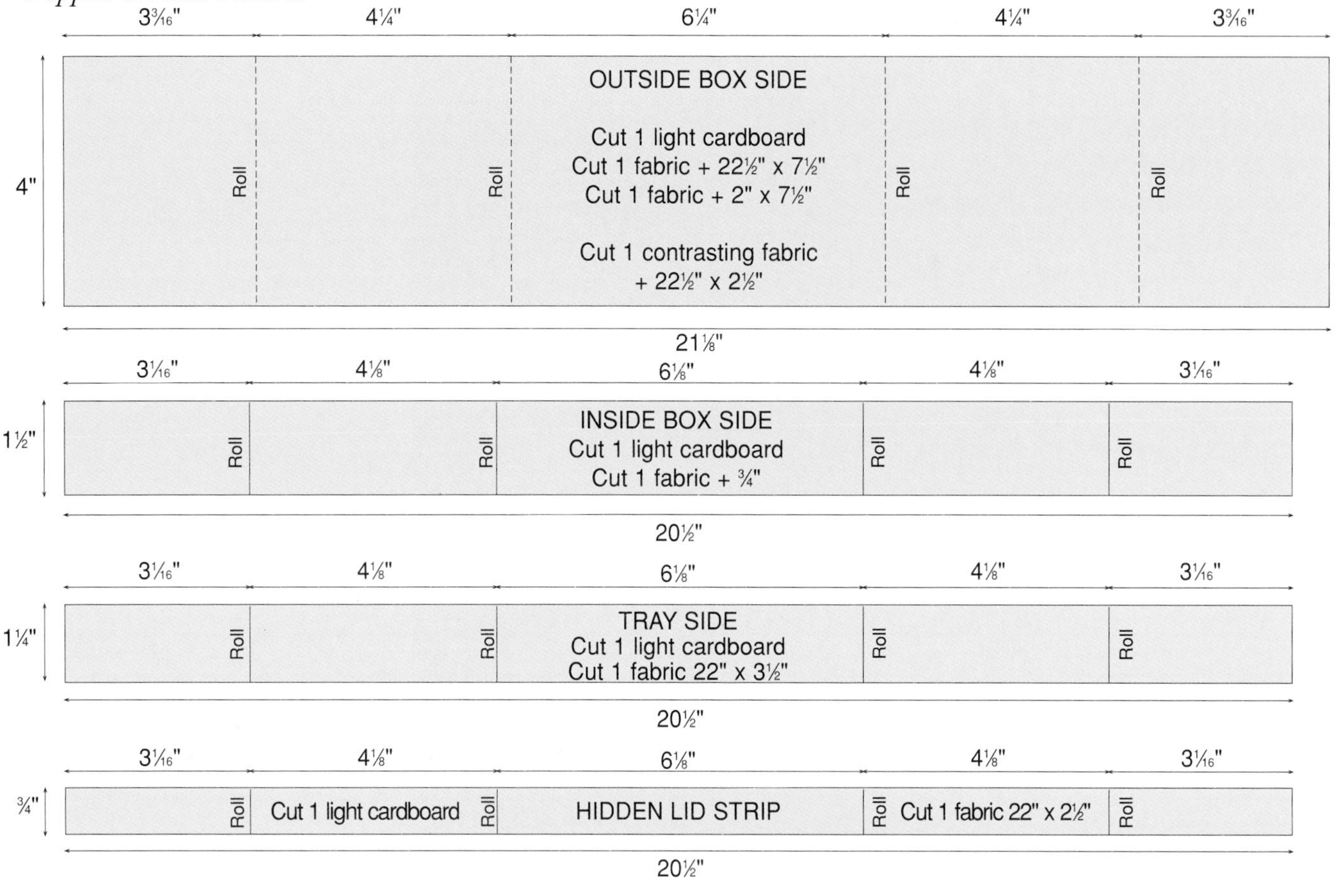
3 3/16"
4 1/4"
6 1/4"
4 1/4"
3 3/16"
4"
OUTSIDE BOX SIDE
Cut 1 light cardboard
Cut 1 fabric + 22 1/2" x 7 1/2"
Cut 1 fabric + 2" x 7 1/2"
Cut 1 contrasting fabric
+ 22 1/2" x 2 1/2"
Roll
Roll
Roll
Roll
21 1/8"
3 1/16"
4 1/8"
6 1/8"
4 1/8"
3 1/16"
1 1/2"
INSIDE BOX SIDE
Cut 1 light cardboard
Cut 1 fabric + 3/4"
Roll
Roll
Roll
Roll
20 1/2"
3 1/16"
4 1/8"
6 1/8"
4 1/8"
3 1/16"
1 1/4"
TRAY SIDE
Cut 1 light cardboard
Cut 1 fabric 22" x 3 1/2"
Roll
Roll
Roll
Roll
20 1/2"
3 1/16"
4 1/8"
6 1/8"
4 1/8"
3 1/16"
3/4"
Roll
Cut 1 light cardboard
Roll
HIDDEN LID STRIP
Roll
Cut 1 fabric 22" x 2 1/2"
Roll
20 1/2"

Cube Boxes

All Boxes

Heavy Cardboard	Light Cardboard
BOX SIDES & BASE BASE and LID (Cut 2) INSIDE LID	HIDDEN LID STRIP

Veggie/Fruit Box

Outside Fabric	Inside Fabric
Strip on outside of box: 11½" x 3¼" BASE and LID + ¾" (Cut 2)	BOX SIDES & BASE (as indicated on pattern) HIDDEN LID STRIP: 2" x 11½" INSIDE LID + ¾"

By-the-Sea Box

Paper
Strip on outside of box: 11½" x 3½" BOX SIDES & BASE (indicated on pattern) HIDDEN LID STRIP: 11½" x 1¼" and 11½" x ¾" BASE and LID + ¾" (Cut 2) INSIDE LID + ¾"

Gentle Images Box

Fabric
BOX SIDES & BASE (indicated on pattern) HIDDEN LID STRIP: 2" x 11½" BASE and LID + ¾" (Cut 2) INSIDE LID + ¾"

Tools & Materials

For Each Box—

Heavy cardboard: 18" x 7"
Light cardboard: 18" x 6"
Heat tool
Foam brushes: 1"
Waterbase markers
Dimensional medium (clear)

Veggie/Fruit Box—

Outside fabric: 4½" x 22" (black cotton)
Inside fabric: 12" x 12" (black geometric cotton print)
Rubber stamps: pumpkin, corn, carrots, lemon, peas
Ink pad (black)
Embossing powder (clear)
Decoupage medium (clear)

By-the Sea Box—

Paper: 9" x 36" (lt. green Japanese mulberry)
Rubber stamps: lighthouse, three different shells
Embossing fluid (sheer pink)
Embossing pen with chiseled tip (clear)
Embossing powders: sandy, green
Découpage medium (antique)

Gentle Images Box—

Fabric: ¼ yd. of 45"-wide (two tone ivory cotton print)
Rubber stamps: tea cup, kitty, umbrella, heart, roses
Embossing fluid (sheer pink)
Embossing powder (gold)
Découpage medium (clear)
Trim: 1½ yds. of 1⁄16"-wide (gold cording); ⅜ yd. of ½"-wide (ivory gimp)

Directions

1. Cut Cardboard, Fabric, or Paper; Score

2. Stamp and Emboss Designs onto Cardboard; Color; Coat with Finishes

Make a template from enlarged Template Pattern on page 37. Trace 15 squares (five for each box) onto shiny side of light cardboard, tracing around the inside and outside edges of the template. Cut out squares.

Refer to Box Making Basics for Stamping & Embossing on page 21. Ink a veggie/fruit stamp with black ink. Center and stamp on inside square on shiny front of one square, then immediately emboss with clear embossing powder. Color stamped design using markers and blending colors as desired. Repeat process using remaining veggie/fruit stamps.

Ink a by-the-sea stamp with embossing fluid. Center and stamp on inside square on shiny front of one square, then immediately emboss with sandy embossing powder. Outline stamped design ⅛" from inside edge of square using embossing pen and making pen line uneven. Immediately emboss pen line with green embossing powder. Tap embossing pen over green pen line and immediately emboss with a light coat of sandy embossing powder. Color stamped design using markers and blending colors as desired. Repeat process using remaining by-the-sea stamps. Use one shell stamp twice.

Ink a gentle images stamp with embossing fluid. Center and stamp on inside square on shiny front of one square, then immediately emboss with gold embossing powder. Color stamped design using markers and blending colors as desired. Repeat process using remaining gentle images stamps.

Using a foam brush, apply a coat of clear découpage medium over veggie/fruit and gentle images stamped designs and a coat of antique découpage medium over by-the-sea stamped designs. Let dry. Following manufacturer's instructions, cover stamped designs with a thorough ⅟₁₆"-thick coat of dimensional medium to just beyond inner traced line. Set aside on a flat surface to dry overnight. Stamped designs must be completely dry before completing boxes.

3. Cover Cardboard with Fabric or Paper; Shape

Refer to Box Making Basics for Laminating on page 9. For veggie/fruit box, place BOX SIDE & BASE on work surface unscored side up. Laminate with inside fabric. Finish top long edge, one short side edge, and bottom edges of BOX SIDE as indicated on pattern. Fold BOX SIDE & BASE on score lines and re-emphasize shape by running a 1" dowel over scores. Join short edges of box side by overlapping tab edge to finished short edge and adjoining cardboard edges together at the corner. Glue fabric tab in place. Fold bottom of box up to meet sides and glue box bottom fabric tabs onto bottom edge of sides, adjoining cardboard edges together.

Laminate INSIDE LID with inside fabric.

Laminate BASE and LID with outside fabric. Laminate outside fabric strip to outside of BOX SIDE. Place strip a scant ⅟₁₆" down from top finished edge of BOX SIDE. Glue extended fabric to underside of assembled box.

For Veggie/Fruit Box and Gentle Images Box, refer to Box Making Basics for Laminating Lid Strip on page 15. Place HIDDEN LID STRIP on work surface unscored side up and laminate.

For By-the-Sea Box, place BOX SIDE & BASE on work surface unscored side up. Laminate with paper. Finish top, long edge, one short edge, and bottom edges of BOX SIDE as indicated on pattern. Fold BOX SIDE & BASE on score lines and re-emphasize shape by rolling a 1" dowel over scores. Join short

edges of box side by over-lapping tab edge to finished short side edge and adjoining cardboard edges together at the corner. Glue paper tab in place. Fold bottom of box up to meet sides and glue box bottom paper tabs onto bottom edge of sides, adjoining cardboard edges.

Laminate paper strip to outside of BOX SIDE. Place strip 1/16" down from top finished edge of BOX SIDE. Glue extended paper to underside of assembled cube.

Laminate INSIDE LID, BASE, and LID with paper.

Place HIDDEN LID STRIP on work surface unscored side up and laminate centered onto 1¼" x 11½" paper strip. Finish two long edges and one short edge. Laminate scored side of HIDDEN LID STRIP with ¾" x 11½" strip of paper, placing strip flush to one long edge.

For Gentle Images Box, place BOX SIDE & BASE on work surface unscored side up. Laminate with fabric. Place cardboard onto fabric as indicated on fabric pattern. Finish one short edge and bottom edges of BOX SIDE. With wrong sides together, glue short edge of extended fabric section over on itself at "slice."

Fold BOX SIDE & BASE on score lines and re-emphasize shape by running a 1" dowel over scores. Join short edges of box side by overlapping tab edge to finished short edge and adjoining cardboard edges together. Glue fabric tab in place. Fold bottom of box up to meet sides and glue box bottom fabric tabs onto bottom edge of

sides, adjoining cardboard edges together.

Fold down and laminate extended fabric section over outside of BOX SIDE. Glue bottom edge of extended fabric section to underside of assembled box.

Laminate INSIDE LID, BASE, and MIDDLE LID with fabric.

Refer to Box Making Basics for Laminating Lid Strip. Place HIDDEN LID STRIP on work surface unscored side up and laminate with fabric.

4. Assemble Box Bottom and Lid

Glue wrong side of BASE to bottom of box.

Join short edge of HIDDEN LID STRIP by overlapping tab edge onto finished edge and adjoining cardboard edges together. Glue tab in place. Slip INSIDE LID into HIDDEN LID STRIP at edge with extended fabric. Glue extended fabric over onto wrong side of INSIDE LID, pulling fabric tight for a snug fit.

Glue wrong side of LID to assembled INSIDE LID/ HIDDEN LID STRIP.

5. Glue Stamped Designs to Box Sides and Lid

Cut ¾" border away from stamped designs. Check for fit. Laminate stamped designs to BOX SIDES and LID.

6. Embellish Gentle Images Box

Use a thin bead of tacky glue to attach cording trim around all four outer edges of box LID.

Glue cording trim to sides and top edges of BOX SIDES. Glue half of gimp trim to bottom edge of box. Wrap and glue other half of gimp trim to underside of box.

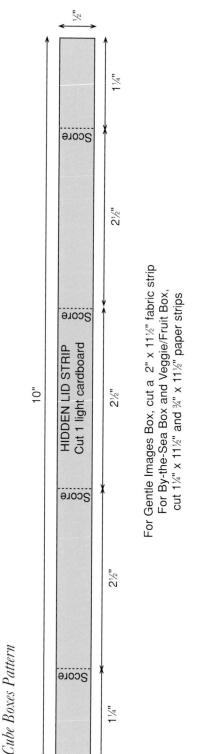

Cube Boxes Pattern

Cube Boxes Patterns   Enlarge 200%

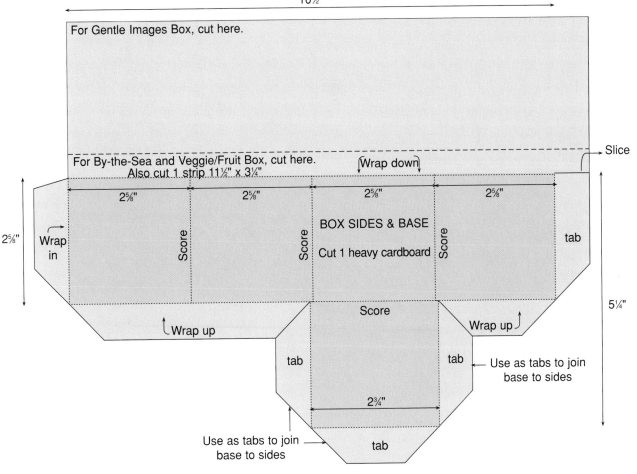

10½"

For Gentle Images Box, cut here.

For By-the-Sea and Veggie/Fruit Box, cut here.
Also cut 1 strip 11½" x 3¼"

Slice

Wrap down

2⅝"   2⅝"   2⅝"   2⅝"

2⅝"

Wrap in

Score   Score   Score

BOX SIDES & BASE

Cut 1 heavy cardboard

tab

5¼"

Score

Wrap up   Wrap up

tab   tab

Use as tabs to join
base to sides

2¾"

Use as tabs to join
base to sides

tab

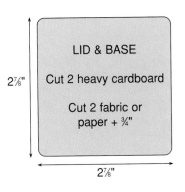

INSIDE LID

Cut 1 heavy cardboard

Cut 1 fabric or
paper + ¾"

2½"

2½"

LID & BASE

Cut 2 heavy cardboard

Cut 2 fabric or
paper + ¾"

2⅞"

2⅞"

Template Pattern   Enlarge 200%

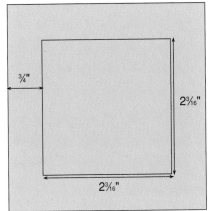

¾"

2³⁄₁₆"

2³⁄₁₆"

Flowers to the fair!
To you these flowers I bring . . .
Flowers sweet, and gay, and delicate like you;
Emblems of innocence, and beauty, too.

—Anna Laefitta Barbauld

Show of Affection 2

Cupcake Boxes

All Boxes

Heavy Cardboard	Light Cardboard
LID and INSIDE LID (Cut 2) BASE INSIDE BOTTOM	OUTSIDE BOX SIDE INSIDE BOX SIDE

Chocolate Cupcake

Box Fabric	Lid Fabric	Lace
OUTSIDE BOX SIDE + ¾" INSIDE BOX SIDE + ¾" INSIDE LID: 3½" circle INSIDE BOTTOM: 2½" circle BASE: 2½" circle	LID: 3½" circle	LID OVERLAY: 3½" circle

Strawberry Cream-filled Cupcake

Box Fabric	Lace
OUTSIDE BOX SIDE + ¾" INSIDE BOX SIDE + ¾" LID and INSIDE LID: 3½" circle (Cut 2) INSIDE BOTTOM: 2½" circle BASE: 2½" circle	LID OVERLAY: 3½" circle

Cupie Cupcake Box

Paper	Inside Fabric	Lid Fabric
OUTSIDE BOX SIDE + ¾" INSIDE BOTTOM: 2½" circle BASE: 2½" circle INSIDE LID: 3½" circle	INSIDE BOX SIDE + ¾"	LID: 3½" circle

Tools & Materials

For Each Box—
Heavy cardboard: 6" x 6"
Light cardboard: 8" square
Masking tape
Needle: hand-sewing
Stuffing
Thread: coordinating

Chocolate Cupcake Box—
Box fabric: 18" x 8" (brown velvet)
Lid fabric: 3½" circle (ivory satin)
Lace: 3½" circle (brown Chantilly)
Silk ribbon: 1¼ yds. of 7mm (brown)
Velvet ribbon: ½ yd. of ³⁄₁₆"-wide (brown)
Wire-edge ribbon: 2½" of ⅞"-wide (red ombré)
Beads: 13 seed (bronze); 3mm round (black)
Needle: beading

Strawberry Cream-filled Cupcake Box—
Box fabric: 18" x 8" (pale rose velvet)
Lace: 3½" circle (ivory Nottingham)
Trims (ivory lace): 12" of ⁵⁄₁₆"-wide scalloped-edge;
½ yd. of ⅝"-wide scalloped-edge
Satin ribbon: 12" of 1"-wide (ivory pleated)
Silk ribbon: 1 yd. of 7mm (variegated ivory)
Wire-edge ribbons: 14" of ⅝"-wide ombré (peach);
9" of ⅝"-wide (mint green)

Cupie Cupcake Box—
Construction paper: 8" x 5" (ivory)
Inside fabric: 9" square (peach print)

Lid fabric: 3½" circle (coordinating peach print)
Trims: 1 yd. each of two coordinating colors (mauve, tan ric-rac); ½ yd. of 1"-wide (ivory scalloped-edge lace)
Button: 1"-wide (ivory)
Rubber stamps: cupie, heart
Ink pad (brown)
Embossing powder (clear)
Heat tool
Pens (mauve, tan)
Découpage medium (antique)
Small sponge brush

Directions
1. Cut Cardboard and Fabric

2. Cover Cardboard with Fabric or Paper; Shape
Refer to Box Making Basics for Laminating on page 9 and laminate OUTSIDE BOX SIDE, INSIDE BOX SIDE, INSIDE BOTTOM, INSIDE LID, and BASE with box fabric. Finish all four edges of OUTSIDE BOX SIDE and INSIDE BOX SIDE.
NOTE: For Cupie Box only, refer to Box Making Basics for Stamping & Embossing on page 21 before proceeding. Evenly stamp cupie three times onto OUTSIDE BOX SIDE, immediately embossing after each impression. Evenly stamp heart 11 times onto top edge of OUTSIDE BOX SIDE, embossing immediately after each impression. Color cupie bodies with tan pen. Add color to cheeks with mauve pen.
Place OUTSIDE BOX SIDE wrong side up on work surface. Beginning at outer short edge, carefully roll with a ½" dowel. Because box has a cone shape, change dowel placement to match flair of box as necessary. Place INSIDE BOX SIDE right side up on work surface and repeat process.
Section and mark LID and lid fabric into quarters. Glue edge of lid fabric to underside edge of LID, matching marks. Ease fabric in between marks to fit LID. Leave one section unglued. Firmly fill with stuffing. Glue remaining section to underside of LID. Overlay lid fabric with lace and glue edge of lace to underside edge of LID. Tuft center of LID to form a slight indentation.

3. Assemble Box Bottom; Embellish
Adjoin short edges of INSIDE BOX SIDE and secure with masking tape. Working upside down, slip INSIDE BOTTOM into assembled INSIDE BOX SIDE. Secure with a thin bead of glue and hold until glue dries.
For Chocolate Cupcake Box, Flute silk ribbon while gluing to underside top edge of INSIDE BOX SIDE. With wrong sides together, wrap and glue OUT-SIDE BOX SIDE to INSIDE BOX SIDE, joining short edges of

OUTSIDE BOX SIDE together and aligning top edges of OUTSIDE BOX SIDE and INSIDE BOX SIDE with each other. Turn box upside down. Flute velvet ribbon while gluing to underside of box bottom. Glue wrong side of BASE to bottom of box.
For Strawberry Cream-filled Cupcake Box, adjoin short edges of OUTSIDE BOX SIDE and secure with masking tape. Place 18" of ⅝"-wide lace trim on work

Cupcake Boxes Patterns Enlarge 125%

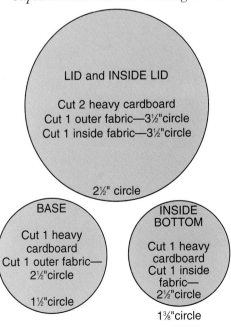

LID and INSIDE LID

Cut 2 heavy cardboard
Cut 1 outer fabric—3½"circle
Cut 1 inside fabric—3½"circle

2½" circle

BASE

Cut 1 heavy cardboard
Cut 1 outer fabric—2½"circle

1½"circle

INSIDE BOTTOM

Cut 1 heavy cardboard
Cut 1 inside fabric—2½"circle

1⅜"circle

surface, wrong side up. Use a 3" disposable roller to cover wrong side of lace trim with a thin layer of thin-bodied tacky glue. Glue lace trim to top outer edge of OUTSIDE BOX SIDE so straight edge of lace trim wraps to inside. Slightly overlap lace trim where cardboard edges adjoin and trim excess away. Glue remaining lace trim to bottom outer edge of OUTSIDE BOX SIDE in the same manner. Glue edge of 5/16"-wide lace trim to top underside edge of INSIDE BOX SIDE. Use a 3" disposable roller to cover underside of INSIDE BOX SIDE with a thin layer of thin-bodied tacky glue. With wrong sides together, slip OUTSIDE BOX SIDE over INSIDE BOX SIDE. Align top edges of OUTSIDE BOX SIDE and INSIDE BOX SIDE. Press together and hold until INSIDE BOX SIDE has bonded to OUTSIDE BOX SIDE. Turn box upside down. Flute silk ribbon while gluing to underside edge on bottom of box. Glue wrong side of BASE to bottom of box.

For Cupie Box, entwine 12" each of tan and mauve ric-rac. Glue one edge of entwined ric-rac to underside top edge of INSIDE BOX SIDE. With wrong sides together, wrap and glue OUT-SIDE BOX SIDE to INSIDE BOX SIDE, adjoining short edges of OUTSIDE BOX SIDE and aligning top edges of OUTSIDE BOX SIDE and INSIDE BOX SIDE with each other. Carefully apply a coat of antique découpage medium to OUTSIDE BOX SIDE. Let dry. Turn box upside down. Glue edge of mauve ric-rac

to underside edge on bottom of box, gathering ric-rac slightly while gluing. Glue wrong side of BASE to bottom of box. Glue tan ric-rac to bottom edge of OUTSIDE BOX SIDE.

4. Assemble Lid; Embellish

For Chocolate Cupcake Box, Flute silk ribbon while gluing to underside edge of LID. With wrong sides together, glue LID to INSIDE LID. Fold wire-edge ribbon in half, matching short edges. Stitch a ¼" seam and finger press seam open. Turn right side out. Gather-stitch along pale red edge. Pull gathers as tightly as possible to form a cup and knot thread. Lightly stuff ribbon cup. Gather-stitch remaining ribbon edge. Pull gathers tightly to form a cherry and knot thread. To make the cherry stem, knot doubled thread on beading needle and insert through center of cherry from light red side. Slip 12 bronze seed beads onto thread and then add one black round bead and one bronze seed bead. Insert needle back through all beads except for the last bronze seed bead that was added. Secure cherry stem on light red under-

side of cherry. Glue cherry to center of LID.

For Strawberry Cream-filled Cupcake Box, Flute silk ribbon while gluing to underside edge of LID. With wrong sides together, glue LID to INSIDE LID. Fold satin ribbon in half, matching short edges. Stitch a ¼" seam and finger press seam open. Gather-stitch along one long selvage edge. Pull gathers as tightly as possible to form a ruffle and knot thread. Glue ruffle to center of LID. Make a Rosette using peach ombré wire-edge ribbon. Make two Folded Leaves using mint green wire-edge ribbon. Glue rosette and leaves to center of ribbon ruffle.

For Cupie Box, glue edge of lace trim to underside edge of LID, slightly gathering lace while gluing. With wrong sides together, glue LID to INSIDE LID. Entwine remaining lengths of ric-rac and join ends together to form a ring. Gather-stitch along one edge of entwined ric-rac. Pull gathers so ring is ¾" in diameter and knot thread. Glue ring to center of LID. Attach button to top of ric-rac ring using industrial-strength glue.

Cupcake Boxes Patterns   Enlarge 200%

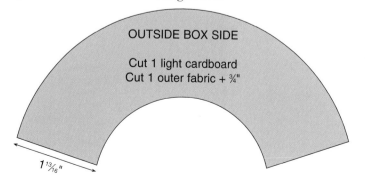

OUTSIDE BOX SIDE

Cut 1 light cardboard
Cut 1 outer fabric + ¾"

1 13/16 "

Cupcake Boxes Patterns   Enlarge 200%

INSIDE BOX SIDE

Cut 1 light cardboard
Cut 1 inside fabric + ¾"

$1\frac{13}{16}$ "

*Our affections
are our life.
We live by them.
They supply our
warmth.*

*—William Ellery
Channing*

Old Charm Basket

Heavy Cardboard	Light Cardboard
BASE and MIDDLE LID (Cut 2)	BOX SIDE A
LID	BOX SIDE B
INSIDE BOTTOM A	
INSIDE BOTTOM B	
INSIDE LID A (Cut 3 each)	
INSIDE LID B (Cut 3 each)	

Two Different Cotton Print Fabrics:		
from one fabric	from second fabric	Solid Fabric
BOX SIDE B: 4" x 22½"	BOX SIDE A: 4" x 17½"	MIDDLE LID + ¾"
INSIDE BOTTOM B + ¾"	INSIDE BOTTOM A + ¾"	LID + ¾"
INSIDE LID B + ¾"	INSIDE LID A + ¾"	
	BASE + ¾"	

Two Shades of Felt:		
from one felt	from second felt	Quilt Batting
Flower basket	4 diamond sections	LID
	5 triangle sections	INSIDE LID A
		INSIDE LID B
		INSIDE BOTTOM A
		INSIDE BOTTOM B

Tools & Materials

Heavy cardboard: 30" x 15"

Light cardboard: 24" x 4"

Cotton fabrics: ½ yd. of 44"-wide (blue checkerboard); ¼ yd. of 44"-wide (two tone dk. blue print); 9" x 24" (black)

Felt: 1 square each (dk. blue, gold)

Quilt batting: ¼ yd.

Trims: 1 yd. of ⅛"-wide (white ric-rac); 1 yd of ½"-wide (white ric-rac)

Embroidery floss: dk. blue, gold, green, red

Cotton ribbons: ½ yd. of 5mm (white); 1 yd. of 9mm (red)

Grosgrain ribbon: 2½ yds. of ⅜"-wide (burgundy)

Silk ribbons: 24" each of 4mm (green, bright green, bright yellow); 1 yd. each of 7mm (lt. green, dk. green synthetic); 2 yds. of 7mm (gold); ¾ yd. each of 13mm (variegated olive green, bright green)

Wire-edge ribbon: 1½" of 1½"-wide (orange ombré)

Picot-edge ribbon: 18" of ¼"-wide (lavender ombré)

Needles: large-eyed darning; hand-sewing; size 20 chenille; size 7 or 8 embroidery

Thread: coordinating

Directions

1. Cut Cardboard and Fabric; Score

2. Piece Basket; Embroider

Center and pin basket to LID fabric. Whip-stitch basket to LID fabric using three strands of dk. blue floss. Pin diamond and triangle sections to basket and Whip-stitch in place using three strands of gold floss.

Couch-stitch basket handle using five strands of red floss. Stitch Lazy Daisies on bottom point of diamonds using three strands of red floss. Stitch Colonial Knots on basket handle and LID fabric using three strands of gold floss.

Enlarge Old Charm Basket Transfer Diagram on page 54 and transfer to right side of pieced basket. Embroider fabric following Old Charm Basket Stitch Guide below and on page 54.

Description	Ribbon/Floss	Stitch
1. Stem	green floss (6 strands)	Outline Stitch
2. Leaves on stem	green silk ribbon bright green silk ribbon	Lazy Daisy
3. Large rose centers	red cotton ribbon	Generous Rose Stitch
4. Large rose	burgundy grosgrain ribbon (nine 2" lengths)	Generous Rose Stitch
5. Daisy	white cotton ribbon	Ribbonwork Daisy
6. Daisy center	orange ombré wire-edge ribbon	Ribbonwork Grape
7. Large leaves	olive green silk ribbon bright green silk ribbon	Pointed Petal Stitch
8. Purple flowers	lavender picot-edge ribbon	Circular Ruffle (three 6" lengths)
9. Purple flower centers	bright yellow silk ribbon	Layered Ribbon Stitches
10. Leaves	lt. green silk ribbon	Pointed Petal Stitch
11. Leaves	dk. green silk ribbon	Ribbon Stitch

3. Cover Cardboard with Fabric; Shape

Refer to Box Making Basics for Laminating Lid Strip on page 15 and laminate unscored side of BOX SIDE B with fabric. Scored side of cardboard is the outside of BOX SIDE B. Fold at each score mark and emphasize scores. Join short edges of BOX SIDE B by overlapping tab edge to finished short edge and adjoining cardboard edges together. Glue tab in place. Fold extending fabric down over scored side of BOX SIDE B. Laminate fabric to scored side. Fabric extends ½" past bottom long edge of BOX SIDE B.

Laminate unscored side of BOX SIDE A with fabric in same manner as BOX SIDE B. Place on work surface unscored side up and roll the middle section with a 1" dowel.

Refer to Box Making Basics for Laminating on page 9 and laminate BASE and MIDDLE LID with fabric. Trim bulk from corners and slash curves and inner corners as necessary.

Glue the three INSIDE LID As together. Glue the three INSIDE LID Bs together.

Refer to Box Making Basics for Padding & Wrapping on page 10 and pad INSIDE BOTTOM A, INSIDE LID A, INSIDE BOTTOM B, and INSIDE LID B with quilt batting, then wrap with fabric.

Pad LID with quilt batting, then carefully center and wrap with embroidered LID fabric, checking often to make certain embroidered basket remains centered on LID.

4. Assemble Box Bottom

Beginning with straight edge, working small sections at a time, and working upside down, glue edge of INSIDE BOTTOM A to bottom edge of BOX SIDE A. Wrap and glue remaining

extended fabric to underside of INSIDE
BOTTOM A. Repeat process for INSIDE
BOTTOM B and BOX SIDE B.

Center and glue straight edge of assembled BOX
BOTTOM A section to center portion of
assembled BOX BOTTOM B section, forming a
basket shape.

5. Embellish Box

Laminate grosgrain ribbon around bottom edge
of box.

Glue edge of ⅛"-wide trim to underside edge of
bottom of box. Glue wrong side of BASE to
bottom of box.

<u>Flute</u> while gluing gold silk ribbon to underside
edges of INSIDE LID A and B. Center and glue
wrong sides of INSIDE LID A and B to right side
of MIDDLE LID.

Glue edge of ½"-wide trim to underside edge of
LID. Gather trim slightly at outward corners to
balance appearance.

With wrong sides together, glue LID to
MIDDLE LID.

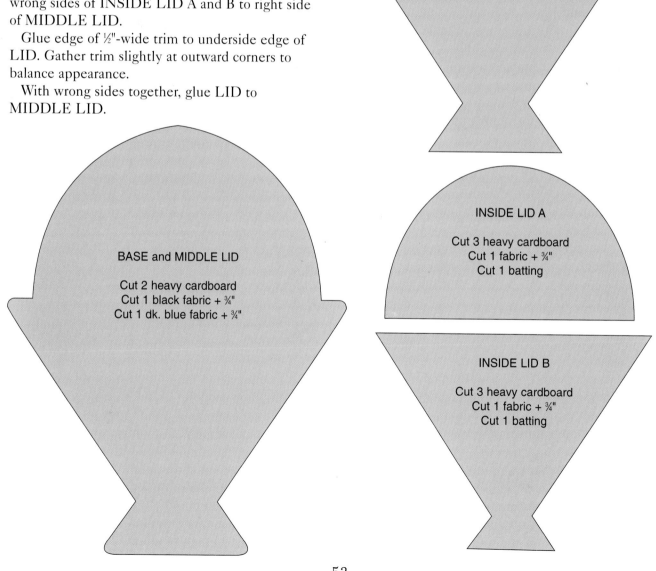

Old Charm Basket Patterns   Enlarge 200%

LID

Cut 1 heavy cardboard
Cut 1 black fabric + ¾"
Cut 1 batting
Cut 1 felt

BASE and MIDDLE LID

Cut 2 heavy cardboard
Cut 1 black fabric + ¾"
Cut 1 dk. blue fabric + ¾"

INSIDE LID A

Cut 3 heavy cardboard
Cut 1 fabric + ¾"
Cut 1 batting

INSIDE LID B

Cut 3 heavy cardboard
Cut 1 fabric + ¾"
Cut 1 batting

Old Charm Basket Patterns   Enlarge 200%

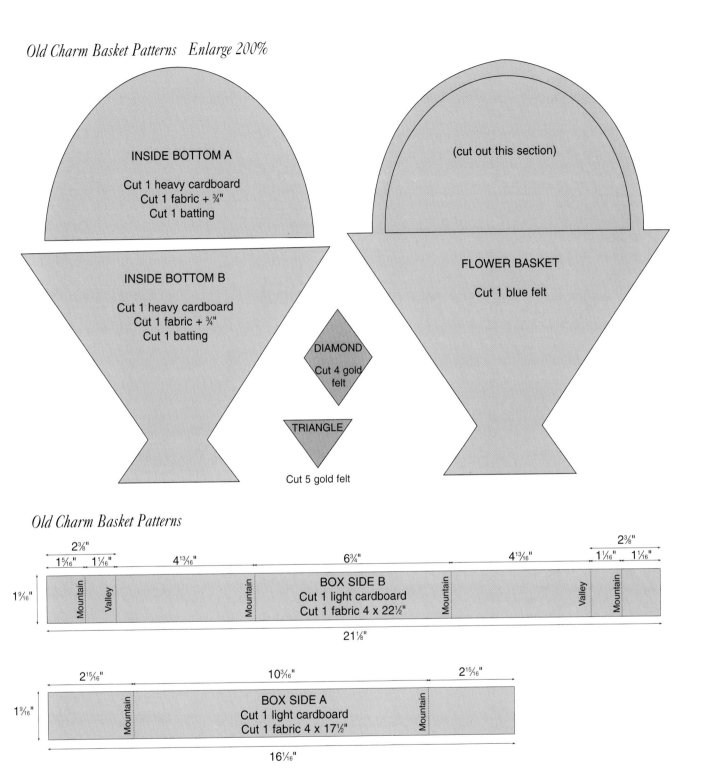

INSIDE BOTTOM A

Cut 1 heavy cardboard
Cut 1 fabric + ¾"
Cut 1 batting

(cut out this section)

FLOWER BASKET

Cut 1 blue felt

INSIDE BOTTOM B

Cut 1 heavy cardboard
Cut 1 fabric + ¾"
Cut 1 batting

DIAMOND
Cut 4 gold felt

TRIANGLE

Cut 5 gold felt

Old Charm Basket Patterns

2⅜"
1⁵⁄₁₆" 1¹⁄₁₆"   4¹³⁄₁₆"   6¾"   4¹³⁄₁₆"   2⅜" 1¹⁄₁₆" 1¹⁄₁₆"

1⁹⁄₁₆"

Mountain Valley   Mountain   **BOX SIDE B**   Mountain   Valley Mountain
                                Cut 1 light cardboard
                                Cut 1 fabric 4 x 22½"

21⅛"

2¹⁵⁄₁₆"   10³⁄₁₆"   2¹⁵⁄₁₆"

1⁹⁄₁₆"

Mountain   **BOX SIDE A**   Mountain
            Cut 1 light cardboard
            Cut 1 fabric 4 x 17½"

16¹⁄₁₆"

In well-cool hollow walk your way, in bee-soft bower sleep you.
In drift, in dream, drink fresh, breathe free; in dream, in home, love keep you.

—*Mary Phelps*

53

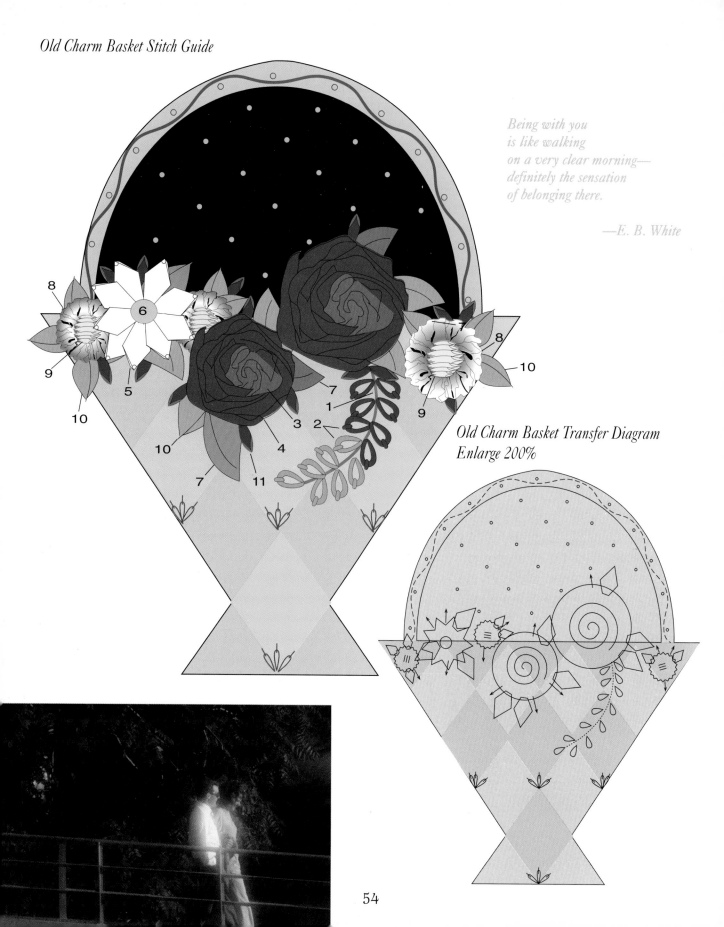

Old Charm Basket Stitch Guide

*Being with you
is like walking
on a very clear morning—
definitely the sensation
of belonging there.*

—E. B. White

8
6
9
5
10
10
7
1
3
2
4
7
11
8
10
9

*Old Charm Basket Transfer Diagram
Enlarge 200%*

3 A Union of Souls

Dresden Plate Box

Heavy Cardboard	Light Cardboard
UPPER BASE	BOX SIDE
MIDDLE LID (cut out center circle) and LOWER BASE (Cut 2)	INNER BOX INSIDE SIDE
	INNER BOX LID STRIP
INSIDE LID (cut out center circle) and INSIDE BOTTOM (Cut 2)	INNER BOX OUTSIDE SIDE
	COMPARTMENT SIDES (Cut 4)
LID SECTIONS (Cut 16)	
COMPARTMENT INSIDE BOTTOMS and BASES (Cut 8)	
INNER BOX LID, INNER BOX INSIDE LID, and INNER BOX BASE (Cut 3)	
INNER BOX INSIDE BOTTOM	

Six Different Cotton Print Fabrics:

from four fabrics	from two fabrics
COMPARTMENT SIDES: 4¼" x 13½" (Cut 1 from each of four fabrics)	INNER BOX INSIDE SIDE: 4½" x 11" (Cut from first fabric)
COMPARTMENT INSIDE BOTTOMS and BASES + ¾" (Cut 2 from each of four fabrics)	INNER BOX INSIDE BOTTOM + ¾"
	INNER BOX INSIDE LID and BASE, + ¾" (Cut 1 from first fabric and cut 1 from second fabric)
LID SECTIONS + ½" (Cut 1 from each of four fabrics)	INNER BOX OUTSIDE SIDE + ¾" (Cut from second fabric)
	INNER BOX LID STRIP: 2¼" x 11½" (Cut from second fabric)
	LID SECTIONS + ½" (Cut 1 from each fabric)

Two Different Small Cotton Print Fabrics:

from one fabric	from second fabric	Pique Fabric
INSIDE BOTTOM + ¾"	INSIDE LID + ¾"	MIDDLE LID + ¾"
LOWER BASE + ¾"	LID SECTION + ½"	UPPER BASE + ¾"
LID SECTION + ½"		INNER BOX LID + ¾"

Large Cotton Print Fabric	Eight Different Cotton Prints	Quilt Batting
BOX SIDE: 5¾" x 26"	LID SECTIONS + ¾" (Cut 1 from each of the eight fabrics)	LID SECTIONS (Cut 16)
		INNER BOX LID
		INSIDE LID

Tools & Materials

Heavy cardboard: 20" x 30"

Light cardboard: 30" x 15"

Cotton fabrics: 6" x 22" in six different prints; 2½" x 4" in eight different prints; 18" x 22" in two different small prints; ¼ yd. of 44"-wide large print

Pique fabric: ⅓ yd. of 44"-wide (white)

Quilt batting: 12" x 15"

Lace: ¾ yd. of ⅞"-wide (blue crocheted)

Wire-edge ribbon: ⅞ yd. of ⅝"-wide (lavender)

Trim: 12" of 1/16"-wide (white ric-rac)

Cotton ribbon: 1¼ yds. of 7mm (lavender)

Silk ribbon: 18" of 13mm (lt. green)

Textured ribbon: 18" of 9mm (lavender)

Button: 1⅛"-diameter coordinating

Needles: chenille size 20; hand-sewing; three large-eyed darning

Thread: coordinating

Directions

1. Cut Cardboard and Fabric; Score

2. Embroider Inner Box Lid Fabric

Embroider a Generous Rose Stitch in center of INNER BOX LID fabric using lavender cotton ribbon for center of rose. Use lavender textured ribbon for outer rose layers. Make three Pointed Petal Stitch near outer edge of rose ruffles using lt. green silk ribbon.

3. Cover Cardboard with Fabric; Shape

Refer to Box Making Basics for Laminating Lid Strip on page 15 and laminate BOX SIDE with large cotton print fabric. Glue ½" of both short edges of fabric. Wrap each short edge over on itself at cardboard edge. Paint uncovered BOX SIDE with glue. Wrap upper fabric onto glued cardboard and smooth completely (this is outside of BOX SIDE). BOX SIDE is now completely covered with fabric and ¾" extends past cardboard's bottom edge. Place on work surface, outside down. Carefully roll with a 1" dowel. Repeat process for INNER BOX LID STRIP using a cotton print fabric.

Refer to Box Making Basics for Laminating on page 9 and laminate INNER BOX OUTSIDE SIDE with a cotton print fabric. Finish all four edges.

Laminate INNER BOX BASE with a cotton print fabric.

Laminate INNER BOX INSIDE SIDE with a cotton print fabric. Place cardboard ⅜" up from one long edge and centered between short edges. Trim bulk from corners and finish all four edges. Do not trim any fabric from top long edge.

Laminate INNER BOX INSIDE LID and INNER BOX INSIDE BOTTOM with a cotton print fabric.

Refer to Box Making Basics for Laminating Lid Strip and laminate unscored side of COMPARTMENT SIDES with cotton print fabrics. Finish one short edge. Place on work surface, covered side up. Fold at each score mark and emphasize scores. Carefully roll the widest section with a 1" dowel. Place on work surface, uncovered side up. Carefully roll the 2⅜"-wide section (right end) with a dowel. Join short edges of COMPARTMENT SIDES by overlapping tab edge to finished short edge and adjoining cardboard edges together. Glue tab in place. Paint uncovered COMPARTMENT SIDES with glue. Turn upper fabric down onto glued cardboard and smooth completely. Fabric extends ¾" past bottom edge of COMPARTMENT SIDES.

Refer to Box Making Basics for Laminating and laminate COMPARTMENT INSIDE BOTTOMS and BASES with a cotton print fabric.

Laminate INSIDE BOTTOM and LOWER BASE with a small cotton print fabric. Clip curves, outward points, and inward corners on LOWER BASE as necessary.

Laminate MIDDLE LID and UPPER BASE with pique fabric. Clip curves, including curves on fabric in center of MIDDLE LID, outward points, and inward corners as necessary.

Refer to Box Making Basics for Padding & Wrapping on page 10 and pad LID SECTIONS with quilt batting, then wrap with cotton print fabrics.

Pad INSIDE LID with quilt batting, then wrap with a small

cotton print fabric. Begin with outer edge. Clip curves, including curves on fabric in center of INSIDE LID, as necessary.

Pad INNER BOX LID with quilt batting, then wrap with pique fabric.

4. Assemble Box Bottom

Wrap BOX SIDE around INSIDE BOTTOM. Hold in place and mark overlap. Overlap and glue one short edge of BOX SIDE to opposite edge at mark. Working upside down, slip INSIDE BOTTOM into BOX SIDE 1/16" down from bottom edge. Glue in place with thin bead of glue. Work small sections at a time and hold until glue dries. Glue extended fabric over onto wrong side of INSIDE BOTTOM, pulling fabric tight for a snug fit.

Glue edge of lace to underside edge of UPPER BASE. With wrong sides together, glue LOWER BASE to UPPER BASE.

Glue bottom of box to right side of UPPER BASE. Glue wire-edge ribbon to bottom edge of BOX SIDE. Glue at ends, and minimally in between. Make a 2"-wide flat bow with remaining ribbon and glue over ends.

5. Assemble Compartments

Working upside down, slip a COMPARTMENT INSIDE BOTTOM into an assembled COMPARTMENT SIDE. Secure with a thin bead of glue. Work small sections at a time and hold until glue dries. Glue extended fabric over onto wrong side of COMPARTMENT INSIDE BOTTOM, pulling fabric tight for a snug fit. Clip curves as necessary.

Glue wrong side of COMPARTMENT BASE to underside of assembled compartment. Repeat process for remaining compartments.

Place compartments into box.

6. Assemble Inner Box

Wrap INNER BOX INSIDE SIDE around INNER BOX INSIDE BOTTOM. Join and assemble as in Step 4 for BOX SIDE and INSIDE BOTTOM.

With wrong sides together, glue INNER BOX OUTSIDE SIDE to INNER BOX INSIDE SIDE. Overlap and glue edges of INNER BOX OUTSIDE SIDE to finish. Flatten glue thoroughly. The INNER BOX INSIDE SIDE stands taller than the INNER BOX OUTSIDE SIDE.

Flute while gluing cotton ribbon to underside edge on bottom of INNER BOX. Glue wrong side of INNER BOX BASE to bottom of INNER BOX.

Wrap INNER BOX LID STRIP around INNER BOX INSIDE LID. Join and assemble lid in same manner as BOX SIDE and INSIDE BOTTOM.

Glue wrong side of INNER BOX LID to assembled lid. Glue trim to edge of INNER BOX LID, covering where INNER BOX LID is glued to assembled lid. Glue button to center of rose.

7. Assemble Lid

Glue wrong side of INSIDE LID to right side of MIDDLE LID.

Glue wrong sides of LID SECTIONS to wrong side of MIDDLE LID, aligning scalloped LID SECTIONS with MIDDLE LID points. Slip assembled lid over inner box to close.

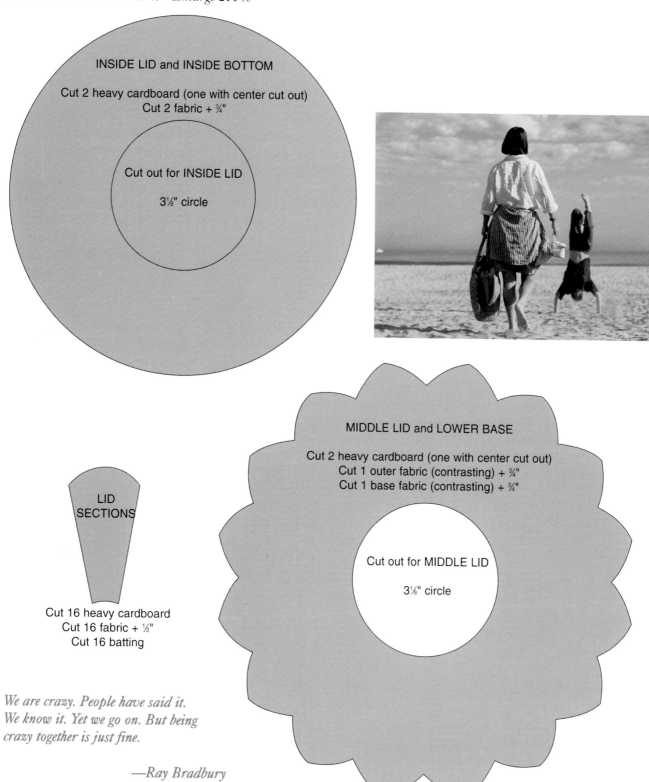

INSIDE LID and INSIDE BOTTOM

Cut 2 heavy cardboard (one with center cut out)
Cut 2 fabric + ¾"

Cut out for INSIDE LID

3⅛" circle

LID
SECTIONS

Cut 16 heavy cardboard
Cut 16 fabric + ½"
Cut 16 batting

MIDDLE LID and LOWER BASE

Cut 2 heavy cardboard (one with center cut out)
Cut 1 outer fabric (contrasting) + ¾"
Cut 1 base fabric (contrasting) + ¾"

Cut out for MIDDLE LID

3⅛" circle

*We are crazy. People have said it.
We know it. Yet we go on. But being
crazy together is just fine.*

—Ray Bradbury

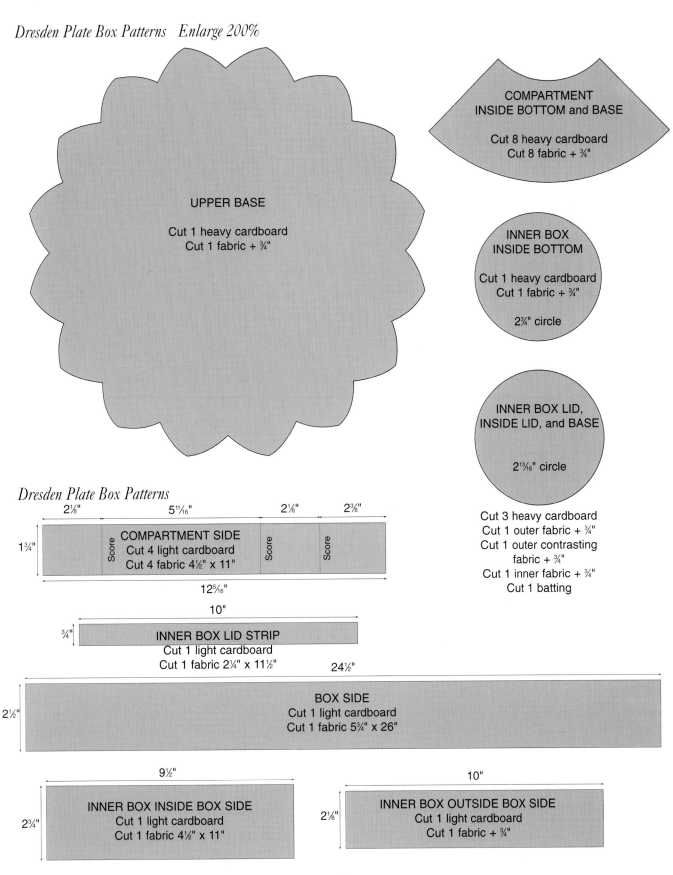

Dresden Plate Box Patterns   Enlarge 200%

UPPER BASE

Cut 1 heavy cardboard
Cut 1 fabric + ¾"

**COMPARTMENT
INSIDE BOTTOM and BASE**

Cut 8 heavy cardboard
Cut 8 fabric + ¾"

**INNER BOX
INSIDE BOTTOM**

Cut 1 heavy cardboard
Cut 1 fabric + ¾"

2¾" circle

**INNER BOX LID,
INSIDE LID, and BASE**

2¹³⁄₁₆" circle

Cut 3 heavy cardboard
Cut 1 outer fabric + ¾"
Cut 1 outer contrasting
fabric + ¾"
Cut 1 inner fabric + ¾"
Cut 1 batting

Dresden Plate Box Patterns

2⅛"   5¹¹⁄₁₆"   2⅛"   2⅜"

1¾"

Score   **COMPARTMENT SIDE**   Score   Score
Cut 4 light cardboard
Cut 4 fabric 4½" x 11"

12⁵⁄₁₆"

10"

¾"

INNER BOX LID STRIP
Cut 1 light cardboard
Cut 1 fabric 2¼" x 11½"

24½"

2½"

BOX SIDE
Cut 1 light cardboard
Cut 1 fabric 5¾" x 26"

9½"

2¾"

INNER BOX INSIDE BOX SIDE
Cut 1 light cardboard
Cut 1 fabric 4½" x 11"

10"

2⅛"

INNER BOX OUTSIDE BOX SIDE
Cut 1 light cardboard
Cut 1 fabric + ¾"

61

Love does not consist in
gazing at each other,
but in looking outward
into the same direction.

—Antoine de Saint-Exupery

We can all talk of
"give and take,"
of what one must
do if one wants
love, of all the
sacrifices one
must make;
but the hardest
thing of all is to
see other persons
as they really are,
and understand
that hearts cannot
be demanded as
a tithe . . . .
And one does not
earn a lover's
wage by giving
love to oneself,
only by giving it to
another.

—Merle Shain

Needlepoint Crest

Heavy Cardboard		Light Cardboard	
LID, INSIDE LID, and BASE (Cut 3; round corners for BASE) INSIDE BOTTOM		OUTSIDE BOX SIDE INSIDE BOX SIDE LID STRIP	

Outside Fabric	Inside Fabric	Quilt Batting
BASE + ¾" OUTSIDE BOX SIDE + ¾" LID STRIP: 3" x 23"	INSIDE BOX SIDE + ¾" INSIDE LID + ¾" INSIDE BOTTOM + ¾"	LID (Cut 2) INSIDE BOTTOM

Tools & Materials

Heavy cardboard: 8" x 30"
Light cardboard: 9" x 24"
Outside fabric: ¼ yd. of 54"-wide (green jacquard)
Inside fabric: ¼ yd. of 54"-wide (plum velvet)
Needlepoint or design fabric: 10" x 10"
Quilt batting: 22" x 9"

Velvet ribbon: ⅔ yd. of ³⁄₁₆"-wide (dk. green)
Wire-edge ribbon: 1½ yds. of ⅞"-wide (plum ombré)
Decorative trim: ⅔ yd. of ⁵⁄₁₆"-wide (plum/green floral garland)

Directions

1. Cut Cardboard and Fabric; Score

2. Cover Cardboard with Fabric; Shape

Refer to Box Making Basics for <u>Laminating</u> on page 9 and laminate unscored side of IN-SIDE BOX SIDE with inside fabric. Finish two long edges and one short edge. Place right side up on work surface. Fold at each score mark and emphasize scores. Carefully roll the two center sections with a 1" dowel. Place INSIDE BOX SIDE wrong side up on work surface. Beginning at outer short edge, carefully roll the two end sections with a 1" dowel.

Laminate scored side of OUTSIDE BOX SIDE with outside fabric. Finish two short edges and one long edge. Unfinished edge is bottom edge of OUTSIDE BOX SIDE. Place wrong side up on work surface. Fold at each score mark and emphasize scores. Remember to fold the ⅜"-wide tab section as well. Carefully roll the two center sections with a 1" dowel. Place OUTSIDE BOX SIDE right side up on work surface. Beginning at outer short edge, carefully roll the two end sections with a 1" dowel. The ⅜"-wide tab section does not need to be rolled.

Refer to Box Making Basics for <u>Laminating Lid Strip</u> on page 15 and laminate unscored side of LID STRIP with outside fabric. Scored side of cardboard is the outside of LID STRIP. Place unscored side up on work surface and shape in same manner as INSIDE BOX SIDE.

Laminate BASE with outside fabric. Laminate INSIDE LID with inside fabric. Trim out all bulk from corners.

Refer to Box Making Basics for Padding & Wrapping on page 10 and pad INSIDE BOTTOM with quilt batting, then wrap with inside fabric. Trim bulk from corners of needlepoint or design fabric. Pad LID with two layers of quilt batting, then wrap with needlepoint or design fabric.

3. Assemble Box Bottom

Refer to Box Making Basics for Assembling Style A Box Side & Bottom on page 12 and assemble INSIDE BOTTOM and INSIDE BOX SIDE, beginning at edge of INSIDE BOTTOM corner point and bottom edge of INSIDE BOX SIDE at center score and working up to top corners of crest. Before proceeding, join short edges of INSIDE BOX SIDE by overlapping tab fabric edge to finished short edge and adjoining cardboard edges. Glue tab in place. Glue remaining edges of INSIDE BOTTOM to INSIDE BOX SIDE.

With wrong sides together and beginning at center front point, glue OUTSIDE BOX SIDE to INSIDE BOX SIDE. Be certain to align bottom cardboard edges. Snugly pull OUTSIDE BOX SIDE while gluing. Work

manageable sections at a time. At center back cardboard tabbed edge, glue tab in place, then glue remaining OUTSIDE BOX SIDE section in place, gluing short edge on top of tabbed edge. Glue extending fabric from bottom edge of OUTSIDE BOX SIDE onto BOX BOTTOM. Trim bulk and clip curves as necessary.

4. Assemble Lid

Working upside down, secure edge of INSIDE LID corner point to trimmed edge of LID STRIP at center score with a thin bead of glue and hold until glue dries. Continue gluing INSIDE LID to LID STRIP, about 1" at a time, up to top corners of crest. Before proceeding, join short edges of LID STRIP by overlapping tab fabric edge to finished short edge and adjoining cardboard edges. Glue tab in place. Glue remaining edges of INSIDE LID to LID STRIP.

Fold extended fabric on LID STRIP down over scored side of LID STRIP. At center back sections where cardboard curves inwardly, laminate LID STRIP fabric to cardboard for a cleaner look. Wrap and glue remaining extended fabric to wrong side of INSIDE LID.

5. Embellish; Complete Box

With wrong sides together, glue LID to INSIDE LID. Beginning at center back, glue trim to edge of LID.

Beginning at center back, glue velvet ribbon to bottom edge of box side. Carefully pull both wires from wire-edge ribbon so ribbon gathers very fully. Pull from both ends to alleviate stress that may occur to wire. Fold ribbon in half, matching gathered edges. Turn bottom of box upside down and glue gathered edges of ribbon to underside edge on bottom of box.

Glue wrong side of BASE to bottom of box.

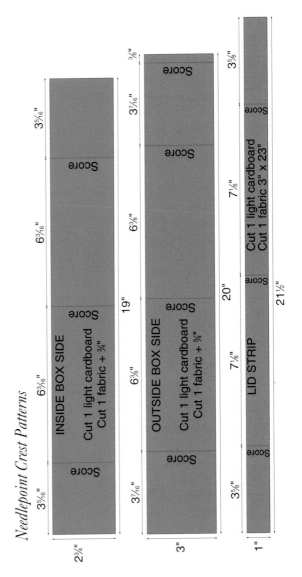

Needlepoint Crest Patterns

INSIDE BOX SIDE
Cut 1 light cardboard
Cut 1 fabric + ¾"

3⁵⁄₁₆" 6³⁄₁₆" 6³⁄₁₆" 3⁵⁄₁₆"
19"
2¾"

OUTSIDE BOX SIDE
Cut 1 light cardboard
Cut 1 fabric + ¾"

3⁄₈" 3⁷⁄₁₆" 6³⁄₈" 6³⁄₈" 3⁷⁄₁₆"
20"
3"

LID STRIP
Cut 1 light cardboard
Cut 1 fabric 3" x 23"

3⁵⁄₈" 7⅛" 7⅛" 3⁵⁄₈"
21½"
1"

Score

65

Needlepoint Crest Pattern Enlarge 200%

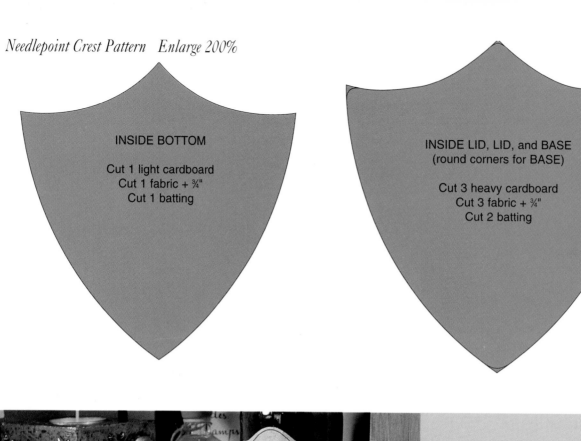

INSIDE BOTTOM

Cut 1 light cardboard
Cut 1 fabric + ¾"
Cut 1 batting

INSIDE LID, LID, and BASE
(round corners for BASE)

Cut 3 heavy cardboard
Cut 3 fabric + ¾"
Cut 2 batting

*Love is a canvas furnished by nature
and embroidered by imagination.*

—Voltaire

Cottage Boxes

All Boxes	
Heavy Cardboard	Light Cardboard
HOUSE INSIDE	HOUSE OUTSIDE
INSIDE BOX BASE	INSIDE BOX OUTSIDE SIDE
INSIDE BOX INSIDE BOTTOM	INSIDE BOX INSIDE SIDE

All Boxes
Paper
HOUSE INSIDE + ¾"
INSIDE BOX BASE + ¾"
INSIDE BOX INSIDE BOTTOM + ¾"
INSIDE BOX INSIDE SIDE + ¾"

Traveling in the company of those we love is home in motion.

—Leigh Hunt

Tools & Materials

For Each Box—
Heavy cardboard: 18" x 5"
Light cardboard: 14" x 8" (shiny side);
  12" x 3" (matte side)
Rubber stamps: Victorian house
Ink pad (brown)
Embossing powder (clear)
Heat tool
Waterbase markers (colors of choice)

Iris Box—
Paper: 36"-wide (white Japanese mulberry)
Rubber stamps: picket fence with roses, iris border

Christmas Box—
Paper: 36"-wide (dk. green Japanese mulberry)
Rubber stamps: Colonial Christmas house,
  "Peace on Earth" animals, forest ridge
Liquid appliqué (white)

Rose Box—
Paper: 36"-wide (burgundy Japanese mulberry)
Rubber stamps: picket fence with roses,
  "She who plants a garden"

Directions

1. Cut Cardboard and Paper; Score
  Score HOUSE OUTSIDE and INSIDE BOX OUTSIDE SIDE on shiny side of light cardboard.

2. Stamp and Emboss Designs onto Cardboard and Color
  Refer to Box Making Basics for Stamping & Emboss on page 21. For Iris Box, center and stamp Victorian house onto shiny front of HOUSE OUTSIDE, then immediately emboss. Repeat process on shiny back of HOUSE OUTSIDE. Stamp picket fence onto sides of HOUSE OUT-SIDE, slightly overlapping onto front and back, and emboss. Stamp iris border on shiny side around entire INSIDE BOX OUTSIDE SIDE, immediately embossing after each impression. Color stamped designs and sky using markers and blending colors as desired.

  For Christmas Box, center and stamp Victorian house onto shiny front of HOUSE OUTSIDE, then immediately emboss. Repeat process on shiny back of HOUSE OUTSIDE. Stamp Colonial Christmas house onto sides of HOUSE OUTSIDE, slightly overlapping onto front and back, and emboss. Center and stamp "Peace on Earth" animals onto "front" and "back" of INSIDE

BOX OUTSIDE SIDE, embossing after each impression. Stamp forest ridge onto sides of INSIDE BOX OUTSIDE SIDE, slightly overlapping onto front and back, and embossing after each impression. Color stamped designs and sky using markers and blending colors as desired. Cover bottom edges of HOUSE OUTSIDE with liquid appliqué. Dot liquid appliqué on sky. Let dry overnight, then heat liquid appliqué with heat tool to make snow puffy.

For Rose Box, center and stamp Victorian house onto shiny front of HOUSE OUTSIDE, then immediately emboss. Repeat process on shiny back of HOUSE OUTSIDE. Center and stamp "She Who Plants a Garden" onto "front" and "back" of INSIDE BOX OUTSIDE SIDE, embossing after each impression. Stamp picket fence onto sides of INSIDE BOX OUTSIDE SIDE, slightly overlapping onto front and back, and emboss. Color stamped designs and sky using markers and blending colors as desired.

5. Cover Cardboard with Paper; Shape

Refer to Box Making Basics for <u>Laminating</u> on page 9 and laminate unscored side of each HOUSE INSIDE with paper. Fold box into shape before glue dries. Finish edges as shown in Diagram 1.

Laminate unscored side of each INSIDE BOX INSIDE SIDE with paper. Fold into shape before glue dries. Finish one long and one short edge of INSIDE BOX INSIDE SIDE.

Laminate each INSIDE BOX BASE and INSIDE BOX INSIDE BOTTOM with paper.

6. Assemble Each House and Inside Box

Fold HOUSE INSIDE into shape. Glue paper tabbed edges over onto finished edges to assemble HOUSE INSIDE. Let dry.

Glue HOUSE OUTSIDE to HOUSE INSIDE while gluing HOUSE OUTSIDE tabs to itself.

Fold INSIDE BOX INSIDE

SIDE into rectangle shape. Glue paper tabbed short edge over onto finished short edge, adjoining cardboard edges together.

Slip INSIDE BOX INSIDE BOTTOM into unwrapped edge of rectangle. Glue extended paper from bottom edge over onto underside of INSIDE BOTTOM.

Beginning with tabbed edge, glue INSIDE BOX OUTSIDE SIDE to INSIDE SIDE.

With wrong side up, glue INSIDE BOX BASE to bottom of inside box.

Diagram 1

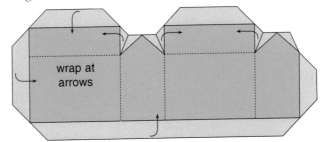

wrap at arrows

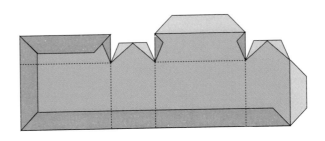

Cottage Boxes Patterns   Enlarge 200%

3¾"
INSIDE BOX INSIDE BOTTOM
Cut 1 heavy cardboard
Cut 1 paper + ¾"

1¾"

4"
INSIDE BOX BASE
Cut 1 heavy cardboard
Cut 1 paper + ¾"

2"

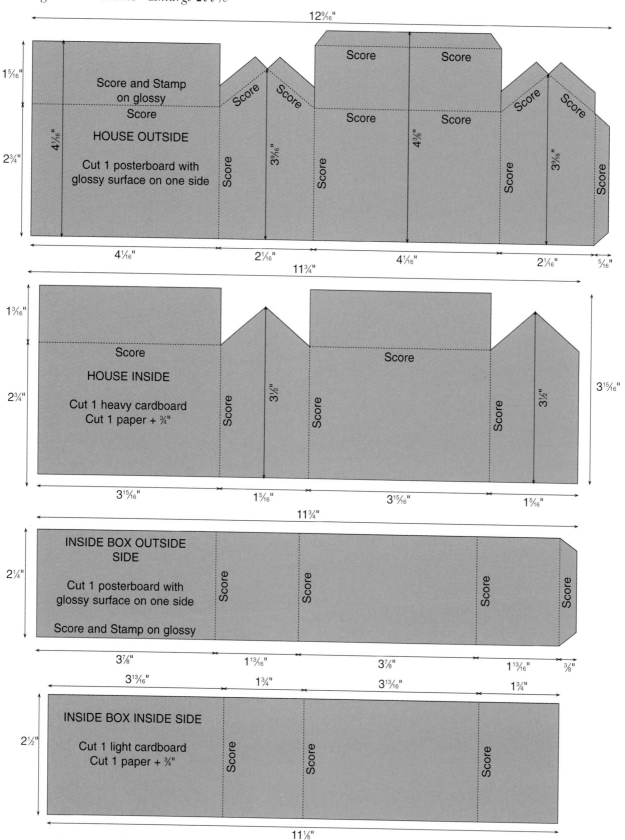

12⁹⁄₁₆"

1⁵⁄₁₆"

2³⁄₄"

Score and Stamp
on glossy
Score

Score

Score

Score

Score

HOUSE OUTSIDE

Cut 1 posterboard with
glossy surface on one side

4¹⁄₁₆"

Score

Score

3⁹⁄₁₆"

Score

Score

4³⁄₈"

Score

Score

Score

Score

3⁹⁄₁₆"

Score

4¹⁄₁₆"

2¹⁄₁₆"

4¹⁄₁₆"

2¹⁄₁₆"

⁵⁄₁₆"

11³⁄₄"

1³⁄₁₆"

2³⁄₄"

Score

HOUSE INSIDE

Cut 1 heavy cardboard
Cut 1 paper + ¾"

Score

3½"

Score

Score

Score

3½"

3¹⁵⁄₁₆"

3¹⁵⁄₁₆"

1⁵⁄₁₆"

3¹⁵⁄₁₆"

1⁵⁄₁₆"

11³⁄₄"

INSIDE BOX OUTSIDE
SIDE

Cut 1 posterboard with
glossy surface on one side

Score and Stamp on glossy

2¼"

Score

Score

Score

Score

3⅞"

1¹³⁄₁₆"

3⅞"

1¹³⁄₁₆"

³⁄₈"

3¹³⁄₁₆"

1¾"

3¹³⁄₁₆"

1¾"

INSIDE BOX INSIDE SIDE

Cut 1 light cardboard
Cut 1 paper + ¾"

2½"

Score

Score

Score

11⅛"

70

Love builds the house on rock
and not sand,
Love laughs what while the winds
rave desperately.

—Christina Rossetti

Felt Flower Boxes

All Boxes
Heavy Cardboard
BOX OUTSIDE
BASE
LID
INSIDE BOTTOM and INSIDE LID (Cut 2)

All Boxes	
Outer Felt	**Inner Felt**
OUTER FABRIC PATTERN	INNER FABRIC PATTERN
	BASE + ½"
	LID + ½"
	INSIDE BOTTOM and INSIDE LID + ½" (Cut 2)
	LID HINGE: 1¾" x 2"
	LID PULL: 3" x ½"

Black-eyed Susan Box		
Pale Yellow Felt	**Gold Felt**	**Dk. Green Felt**
SCALLOPED PATTERN for outer petal layer	POINTED PATTERN for black-eyed Susan center	LEAF (Cut 2)

Aster Box		
Lavender Felt	**Purple Felt**	**Dk. Green Felt**
SCALLOPED PATTERN for outer petal layer	SCALLOPED PATTERN for flower center layer	LEAF (Cut 2)

Rose Box		
Rose Felt	**Bright Pink Felt**	**Blue Green Felt**
SCALLOPED PATTERN for outer petal layer	SCALLOPED PATTERN for flower center layer	LEAF (Cut 2)

Pansy Box			
Dk. Purple Felt	**Lavender Felt**	**Purple Felt**	**Green Felt**
PANSY A (Cut 2)	PANSY B (Cut 2)	PANSY A (Cut 1)	LEAF (Cut 3)

There is a glory in tree and blossom, a trill in the wild bird's tone,
A balm in the summer breezes, that love revealeth, alone.
—Benjamin S. Parker

Cornflower Box		
Blue Felt	Dk. Blue Felt	Dk. Green felt
SCALLOPED PATTERN for outer petal layer	SCALLOPED PATTERN for flower center layer	LEAF (Cut 2)

Tools & Materials
For Each Box—
Heavy cardboard: 22" x 5"
Outside felt: 4" x 14"
Inside felt: 27" x 7"
Outer petal felt: 13" x 2"
Center petal felt: 13" x 1½"
Leaf felt: 3½" x 2½" (for each)
Pansy petals: 3" squares
Buttons: four ¾" (black velvet)

Needle: hand-sewing
Pinking shears
Thread: coordinating

Felt Flower Boxes Patterns

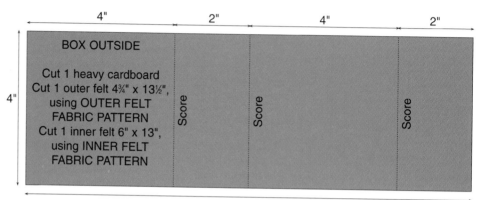

Directions

1. Cut Cardboard and Felt; Score

2. Cover Cardboard with Fabric; Shape
Refer to Box Making Basics for Laminating on page 9 and laminate unscored side of BOX OUTSIDE with inner felt. Place cardboard as shown on INNER FELT FABRIC PATTERN. Trim felt from two short edges and one long edge as indicated on fabric pattern.

Laminate scored side of BOX OUTSIDE with outer felt. Place cardboard as shown on OUTER FELT FABRIC PATTERN. Trim felt from one short edge as indicated on fabric pattern. Let dry 5 minutes, then fold BOX OUTSIDE on score lines.

Laminate BASE, LID, INSIDE BOTTOM, and INSIDE LID with felt. Trim all bulk.

3. Assemble Box
Fold box into rectangle shape. Invisibly glue short edges together, then wrap and glue scalloped edge of outer felt over to backside of rectangle.

Fold scalloped "cuff" of inner felt down over outer felt. Glue cuff tab onto box side. Glue finished scalloped edge over tab. This is top edge of box.

Slip INSIDE BOTTOM 1/16" down from bottom edge of assembled rectangle box. Glue in place. Glue fabric that extends past bottom edge of box to underside of INSIDE BOTTOM.

Center and glue wrong side of BASE to bottom of box.

Place LID on work surface wrong side up and roll with a 1" dowel. Place INSIDE LID on work surface right side up and roll with a 1" dowel.

Fold ½" x 3"-wide felt strip in half, matching short edges. Glue together at ends. Center and glue ½" of folded felt strip to an underside short edge of INSIDE LID. Glue half of the 2" x 1¾"-wide felt hinge piece at opposite underside short edge of INSIDE LID.

With wrong sides together, glue LID to INSIDE LID.

Glue remaining portion of felt hinge to left side inside side of box about ⅝" down from top edge of box.

4. Make Flowers and Leaves
For Black-eyed Susan Box, and with ⅛" intervals, fringe-clip scalloped-edge of pale yellow felt strip. Gather-stitch fringed strip along straight edge. Pull gathers as tightly as possible and knot thread. Join ends together.

Gather-stitch straight edge of gold pointed-edge felt strip. Pull gathers as tightly as possible and knot thread. Join ends and adjust gathers. Glue gold petal layer over pale yellow petal layer. Glue button to center of petals. Glue black-eyed susan to box at center front top edge.

For Aster Box, and with ⅛" intervals, fringe-clip scalloped edges of purple and lavender felt strips. Gather-stitch and assemble in same manner as black-eyed susan. Glue button to center of petals. Glue aster to box at center front top edge.

For Rose Box, gather-stitch along straight edge of rose felt strip. Pull gathers as tight as possible and knot thread. Join ends and adjust gathers. Stitch bright pink felt strip into a <u>Gathered Rose</u>. Glue petal layers together. Glue rose to box at center front top edge.

For Pansy Box, gather-stitch pansy petals together along straight edges in following sequence: lavender B, purple A, lavender B, dk. purple A, dk. purple A. Pull gathers as tight as possible and knot thread. Join ends and adjust and shape petals. Glue button to center of petals. Glue pansy to box at center front top edge.

For Cornflower Box, gather-stitch along straight edge of blue felt strip. Pull gathers as tight as possible and knot thread. Join ends and adjust and shape petals. With ⅛" intervals, fringe-clip scalloped edge of dk. blue felt strip. Gather-stitch in same manner as aster. Glue petal layers together. Glue button to center of

petals. Glue cornflower to box at center front top edge.

For leaves on all boxes, trim sides of leaves with pinking

shears. Gather-stitch along straight edge of leaves. Pull gathers tight and knot thread. Glue leaves to box underneath petals.

Felt Flower Boxes Patterns   Enlarge 145%

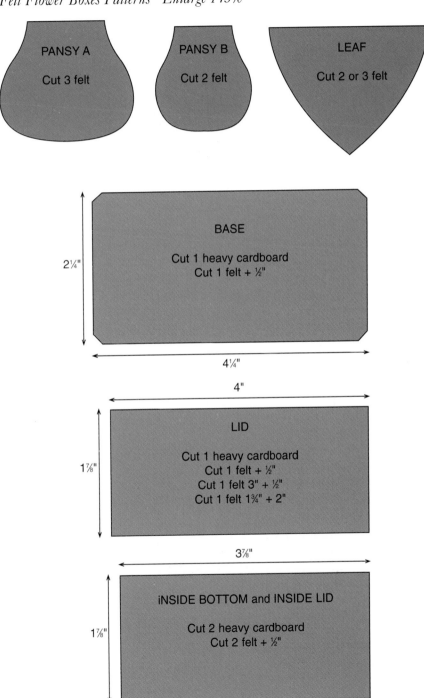

PANSY A

Cut 3 felt

PANSY B

Cut 2 felt

LEAF

Cut 2 or 3 felt

BASE

Cut 1 heavy cardboard
Cut 1 felt + ½"

2¼"

4¼"

4"

LID

Cut 1 heavy cardboard
Cut 1 felt + ½"
Cut 1 felt 3" + ½"
Cut 1 felt 1¾" + 2"

1⅞"

3⅞"

iNSIDE BOTTOM and INSIDE LID

Cut 2 heavy cardboard
Cut 2 felt + ½"

1⅞"

Felt Flower Boxes Patterns   Enlarge 200%

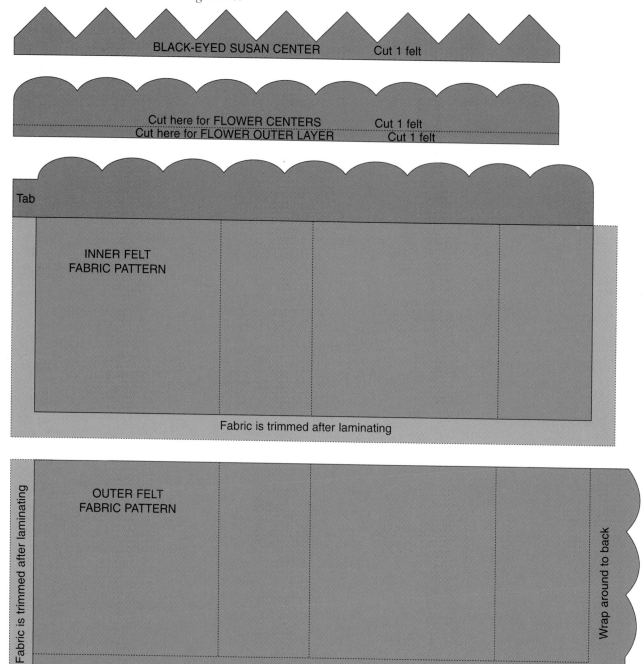

BLACK-EYED SUSAN CENTER   Cut 1 felt

Cut here for FLOWER CENTERS   Cut 1 felt
Cut here for FLOWER OUTER LAYER   Cut 1 felt

Tab

INNER FELT
FABRIC PATTERN

Fabric is trimmed after laminating

OUTER FELT
FABRIC PATTERN

Fabric is trimmed after laminating

Wrap around to back

Wrap around to underside

No love, no friendship can cross the path of our destiny without leaving some mark on it forever.

—François Mauriac

4 Nurturing Love

Growing Garden Box

Heavy Cardboard	Light Cardboard
LID and INSIDE LID (Cut 2)	OUTSIDE SIDE A (Cut 4)
MIDDLE LID	OUTSIDE SIDE B (Cut 4)
BASE	INSIDE SIDE A (Cut 4)
INSIDE BOTTOM	INSIDE SIDE B (Cut 4)

Three Different Cotton Print Fabrics:

from one fabric	from second fabric	from third fabric
MIDDLE LID + ¾"	OUTSIDE SIDE B	INSIDE LID + ¾"
BASE + ¾"	+ ¾" (Cut 4)	INSIDE BOTTOM + ¾"
OUTSIDE SIDE A		INSIDE SIDE A + ¾" (Cut 4)
+ ¾" (Cut 4)		INSIDE SIDE B + ¾" (Cut 4)
		LID HINGE: 4" x 3"

Quilt batting	Cross-Stitch Fabric
LID (Cut 2)	LID + ¾"
OUTSIDE SIDE A (Cut 4)	
OUTSIDE SIDE B (Cut 4)	
INSIDE LID	
INSIDE BOTTOM	
INSIDE SIDE A (Cut 4)	
INSIDE SIDE B (Cut 4)	

Tools & Materials

Heavy cardboard: 7" x 30"

Light cardboard: 9" x 20"

Cotton fabrics (to coordinate with cross-stitch design): 9" x 22" (green garden print); 5" x 16" (green check); ¼ yd. of 44"-wide (lt. green garden print)

Aida cloth: 10" x 10" 16 count

Quilt batting: ¼ yd. of 44"-wide

Trim: 1¼ yds. of ½"-wide (dk. aqua ric-rac)

Cotton ribbons (bright pink): 2 yds. of 9mm; 1½ yds. of 5mm

Silk ribbon: 2 yds. of 7mm (pink)

Grosgrain ribbon: 2 yds. of 9mm (bright green)

Embroidery floss: DMC color numbers 310, 335, 3326, 3712, 3761, 3819, 433, 725, 758, 792, 913, white for cross-stitch; coordinating color for box construction (dk. aqua)

Needles: size 20 chenille; three large-eyed darning; embroidery; hand-sewing

Thread: coordinating

Directions

1. Cross-stitch LID following Growing Garden Box Stitch Guide and Chart on pages 80 and 81.

2. Cut Cardboard and Fabric

3. Embroider Outside Side Fabric
   Embroider each OUTSIDE SIDE A green garden print fabric with a <u>Generous Rose Stitch</u> using silk ribbon for center of each rose. Use cotton ribbon for outer rose layers. Make three <u>Pointed Petal Stitches</u> for each rose near outer edge of rose ruffles using grosgrain ribbon.

4. Cover Cardboard with Fabric; Shape

Refer to Box Making Basics for <u>Laminating</u> on page 9 and laminate MIDDLE LID and BASE with green garden print fabric.

Refer to Box Making Basics for <u>Padding & Wrapping</u> on page 10 and pad each OUTSIDE SIDE A with quilt batting, then center and wrap with embroidered fabric.

Pad each OUTSIDE SIDE B with quilt batting, then wrap with green check fabric.

Pad each INSIDE SIDE A and B with quilt batting, then wrap with lt. green garden print fabric.

Pad INSIDE LID and INSIDE BOTTOM with quilt batting, then wrap with lt. green garden print fabric.

Pad LID with two layers of quilt batting, then wrap with cross-stitch design.

Place each OUTSIDE BOX SIDE A and B wrong side up on work surface. Beginning at a straight edge, roll each piece with a ½" dowel. Place each INSIDE BOX SIDE A and B right side up on work surface. Beginning at a straight edge, roll each piece with a ½" dowel.

5. Assemble Box Bottom

Use doubled, coordinating thread to hand whip-stitch each OUTSIDE SIDE A and B together at curved edges. Make certain to securely and invisibly knot thread at beginning and ending of "seams." Use three strands of dk. aqua embroidery floss to whip-stitch over thread seams.

Working upside down, slip INSIDE BOTTOM into assembled outside side. Secure with a thin bead of glue. Work small sections at a time and hold until glue dries.

Fold LID HINGE fabric over ½" on each 3" side and press. Fold LID HINGE fabric in half, matching pressed edges. Stitch or glue pressed edges together. Glue one long edge of LID HINGE fabric to wrong side top edge of an OUTSIDE SIDE A.

With wrong sides together, align and glue INSIDE SIDE As and Bs to OUTSIDE SIDE As and Bs.

Use three strands of dk. aqua embroidery floss to whip-stitch over top edge of box bottom. Do not stitch hinged edge.

Glue edge of trim to underside edge on bottom of box. Glue wrong side of BASE to bottom of box.

6. Assemble Lid; Complete Box

Measure a generous ⅛" above top edge of box inside onto LID HINGE and mark. Glue edge of wrong side of INSIDE LID to mark on LID HINGE. Close INSIDE LID over box bottom to make certain hinge is not binding. Glue right side of MIDDLE LID to wrong side of INSIDE LID.

Use three strands of dk. aqua embroidery floss to whip-stitch around outer edge of LID.

<u>Flute</u> while gluing cotton ribbon to underside edge of LID. Glue edge of trim to underside edge of LID so half of trim is fully visible. With wrong sides together, glue LID to MIDDLE LID.

Growing Garden Box Stitch Guide

Stitched on white Cashel linen 28 over two threads, the finished design size is 5" x 5". The fabric was cut 8" x 8".

Other Fabrics	Design Size
Aida 11	6⅜" x 6⅜"
Aida 18	3⅞" x 3⅞"
Hardanger 22	3⅛" x 3⅛"
Linen 32 over 2	4⅜" x 4⅜"

Stitch count: 70 x 70

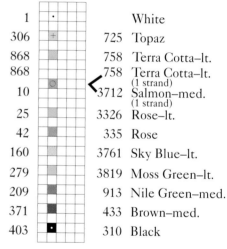

Anchor		DMC	
		Step 1:	**Cross Stitch (2 strands)**
1	·		White
306	+	725	Topaz
868		758	Terra Cotta–lt.
868		758	Terra Cotta–lt. (1 strand)
10	○	3712	Salmon–med. (1 strand)
25		3326	Rose–lt.
42		335	Rose
160		3761	Sky Blue–lt.
279		3819	Moss Green–lt.
209		913	Nile Green–med.
371		433	Brown–med.
403	■	310	Black

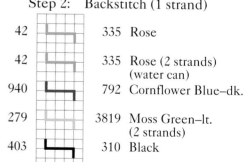

Anchor		DMC	
		Step 2:	**Backstitch (1 strand)**
42		335	Rose
42		335	Rose (2 strands) (water can)
940		792	Cornflower Blue–dk.
279		3819	Moss Green–lt. (2 strands)
403		310	Black
		Step 3:	**French Knot (1 strand)**
403	●	310	Black

Growing Garden Box Stitch Chart

Growing Garden Box Patterns *Enlarge 200%*

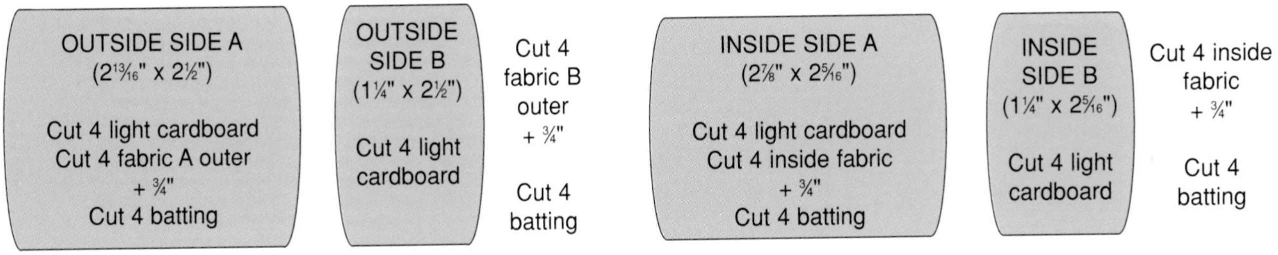

| OUTSIDE SIDE A (2¹³⁄₁₆" x 2½") Cut 4 light cardboard Cut 4 fabric A outer + ¾" Cut 4 batting | OUTSIDE SIDE B (1¼" x 2½") Cut 4 light cardboard | Cut 4 fabric B outer + ¾" Cut 4 batting | INSIDE SIDE A (2⅞" x 2⁵⁄₁₆") Cut 4 light cardboard Cut 4 inside fabric + ¾" Cut 4 batting | INSIDE SIDE B (1¼" x 2⁵⁄₁₆") Cut 4 light cardboard | Cut 4 inside fabric + ¾" Cut 4 batting |

4⅝"

LID and INSIDE LID

Cut 2 heavy cardboard
Cut 1 inside fabric + ¾"
Cut 1 inside fabric 4" x 3"
Work 1 cross-stitch
Cut 3 batting

4⅝"

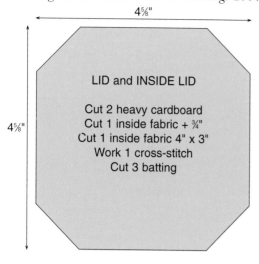

5"

BASE

Cut 1 heavy cardboard
Cut 1 fabric A outer + ¾"

5"

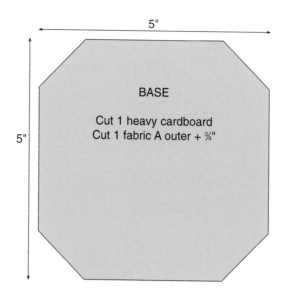

5⅛"

MIDDLE LID

Cut 1 heavy cardboard
Cut 1 fabric A outer + ¾"

5⅛"

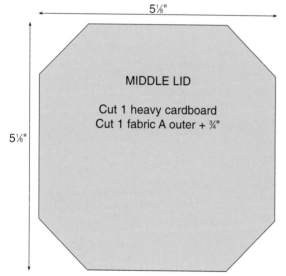

4¾"

INSIDE BOTTOM

Cut 1 heavy cardboard
Cut 1 inside fabric + ¾"
Cut 1 batting

4¾"

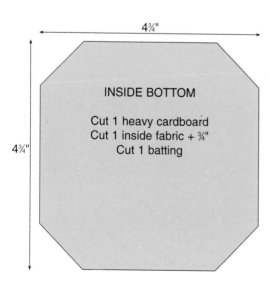

Floral Cat's Eye

Heavy Cardboard	Light Cardboard
BASE and MIDDLE LID (Cut 2)	BOX SIDE
LID	LINING STRIP
INSIDE BOTTOM	
INSIDE LID	

Velveteen Fabric	Silk Fabric
BOX SIDE + ¾"	INSIDE BOTTOM LINING
BASE and MIDDLE LID + ¾" (Cut 2)	INSIDE LID + ¾"
LID + ¾"	

Quilt Batting
LID (Cut 2)
INSIDE BOTTOM

Love is the only flower that grows and blossoms without the aid of seasons.

—Kahlil Gibran

Tools & Materials
Heavy cardboard: 30" x 9"
Light cardboard: 6" x 20"
Velveteen fabric: ¼ yd. of 44"-wide (pearl)
Silk fabric: 22" x 15" (khaki green)
Lace: a variety of vintage pieces
Quilt batting: 9" x 18"

Trim: 1¼ yds. of ½"-wide (ivory lace)
Velvet ribbon: 1¼ yds. of ³⁄₁₆"-wide (ivory)
Wire-edge ribbons: 2 yds. of ⅞"-wide (dusty lilac);
  1 yd. of ⅞"-wide (mauve ombré); 3" of 1½"-wide
(ecru); ½ yd. of 1½"-wide (dk. green)
Lettuce-edge ribbon: ¾ yd. of ½"-wide (mauve)
Grosgrain ribbons: ⅝ yd. each of ⅜"-wide (plum, ecru)
Silk ribbons: 12" each of 4mm (taupe, gold); 1¼ yds.
  of 4mm (plum); 1½ yds. of 7mm (dusty green);
  1 yd. of 13mm (lt. green)
Textured ribbon: 3 yds. of 7mm (dk. green cross-dyed)
Embroidery floss (ecru)
Beads: 30 miniature (pearl)

Directions
1. Cut Cardboard and Fabric; Score

2. Cover Cardboard with Fabric
  Refer to Box Making Basics for <u>Laminating</u> on page 9 and laminate scored side of BOX SIDE, BASE, and MIDDLE LID with velveteen fabric. Finish all four edges of BOX SIDE, trimming bulk from corners.
  Carefully laminate lace to left center front of BOX SIDE. Wrap and glue edge around to inside top edge. Position lace on right end of BOX SIDE near center front. Wrap and glue edges to underside. Place BOX SIDE on work surface wrong side up. Fold at each score line to emphasize shape and roll with a 1" dowel.
  Refer to Box Making Basics for <u>Padding & Wrapping</u> on page 10 and pad LID with two layers of quilt batting, then wrap with velveteen fabric. Position laces on LID and wrap edges to underside.
  Pad and wrap INSIDE LID with silk fabric.

3. Assemble Ribbonwork and Attach to LID and BOX SIDE
  Enlarge Floral Cat's Eye Transfer Diagrams on pages 86 and 87 and transfer to right side of fabric for LID and BOX SIDE. Assemble flowers and leaves and embroider fabric following Floral Cat's Eye Stitch Guide on opposite page and page 87.

Description	Ribbon/Floss	Stitch
1. Wild Rose	mauve ombré wire-edge ribbon (twelve 2½" lengths)	Wild Rose
2. Stamens	taupe and gold silk ribbon (six 2" lengths)	Knotted Petals
3. Small Roses	mauve lettuce-edge ribbon (three 9" lengths)	Gathered Rose (Make 3)
4. Hydrangea	dusty lilac wire-edge ribbon (sixteen 4" lengths)	Hydrangea (Make 16)
5. Hydrangea Centers	ecru floss (6 strands)	Colonial Knot
6. Daisies	ecru grosgrain ribbon (seven 2" lengths)	Ribbonwork Daisy
7. Daisies	plum grosgrain ribbon (ten 2" lengths)	Ribbonwork Daisy (Make 2)
8. Leaves	dk. green wire-edge ribbon	Folded Leaves (Make 3)
9. Leaves	lt. green silk ribbon	Ruffled Ribbon Stitch
10. Leaves	dk. green textured ribbon	Pointed Petal Stitch
11. Leaves	dusty green silk ribbon	Ribbon Stitch
12. Cascading	plum silk ribbon	Cascading Stitch (Use 27" for LID. Use 36" for BOX SIDE.)
13. Beading	pearls	Beading Stitch

Construct flowers and leaves following Special Ribbonwork Instructions below and glue to LID and BOX SIDE. Embroider remaining ribbon stitches through cardboard. It is not difficult to embroider through the cardboard and stitch placement is easier. For LID, once needle is inserted through cardboard, travel from one stitch to the next just below the surface of the fabric.

Special Ribbonwork Instructions:

Wild Rose — Cut twelve 2½" lengths. Fold and stitch each ribbon as shown in Diagram 1. Turn petals right side out. Chain gather-stitch four of the petals together as shown in Diagram 2 for rose center. Knot thread and join first petal to last. Chain gather-stitch remaining 8 petals together. Knot thread and join first petal to last. Stitch or glue 4-petal layer over 8-petal layer.

Diagram 1

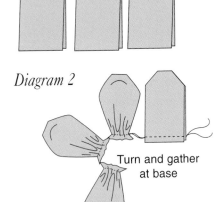

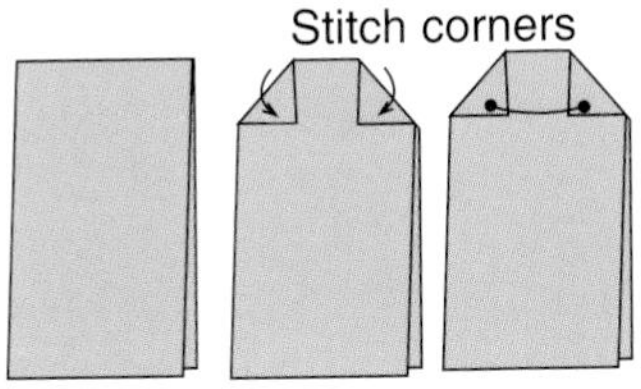

Diagram 2

Turn and gather at base

Stamens — Cut six 2" lengths from each ribbon. Tie knot at center of each ribbon. Chain gather-stitch ribbons together making <u>Knotted Petals</u>. Glue stamens to center of wild rose.

Hydrangea — Cut sixteen 4" lengths. Remove wire from both edges of all ribbons. Fold ribbons in half and gather-stitch as shown in Diagram 3. Pull thread as tightly as possible and knot thread. Fold in half and join ends together at seam. Open out and shape.

Diagram 3

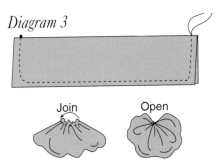

Join   Open

Use six strands of ecru floss to stitch a <u>Colonial Knot</u> in center of each hydrangea.

Daisies — Cut seven 2" lengths from ecru grosgrain. Fold each ribbon in same manner as a <u>Folded Leaf</u>. Press for a crisp point. Chain gather-stitch seven petals together and knot thread. Do not join ends. Trim seam to ⅛". Cut ten 2" lengths from plum grosgrain. Fold and press as before. Chain gather-stitch two sets of five petals together and knot thread. Do not join ends.

Leaves — Make three <u>Folded Leaves</u>. Twist leaf to form a pointed tip. Cut an 18" length from lt. green silk ribbon and knot end. Using a darning needle, stitch through cardboard at leaf location. Measure 2" from entry point. Hand gather-stitch along selvage edge to mark. Pull stitches to gather ribbon and knot thread. Stitch through ribbon and fabric/cardboard in same manner as a <u>Ribbon Stitch</u>.

4. Assemble Box Bottom

Working upside down, and beginning at a corner point, glue edge of INSIDE BOTTOM to edge of BOX SIDE, ¹/₁₆" down from bottom edge of BOX SIDE. Hold in place until glue dries.

Working small sections at a time, continue gluing edge of INSIDE BOTTOM to BOX SIDE front edge.

Glue left side of BOX SIDE back edge to INSIDE BOTTOM. Overlap remaining BOX SIDE over left BOX SIDE back and mark over-lap. Glue right edge over left edge. Glue remaining section of INSIDE BOTTOM to BOX SIDE.

For ribbon hinge, glue edge of ecru wire-edge ribbon to top inside edge of BOX SIDE at center back overlap.

5. Line Box Bottom; Assemble Lid

Refer to Box Making Basics for Lining Boxes on page 13 and line box. Beginning at center front of box, glue LINING STRIP to top inside edge of BOX SIDE, placing strip a scant ⅛" down from top edge.

Rest INSIDE LID right side down over lined box. Glue ribbon hinge onto INSIDE LID (wrong side is facing up), making certain hinge does not bind lid.

Glue wrong side of INSIDE LID to right side of MIDDLE LID.

6. Embellishing

Finger-gather while gluing trim to underside edge of bottom of box. Glue wrong side of BASE to bottom of box.

Flute while gluing velvet ribbon to underside edge of LID. With wrong sides together, glue LID to MIDDLE LID.

There is so much friendship in love, and so much love in friendship, that it would be futile to ask where friendship ends and where love begins.

—Elizabeth Selden

Floral Cat's Eye BOX SIDE Transfer Diagram   Enlarge 230%

Floral Cat's Eye LID Transfer Diagram   Enlarge 170%

Floral Cat's Eye LID Stitch Guide

Floral Cat's Eye BOX SIDE Stitch Guide

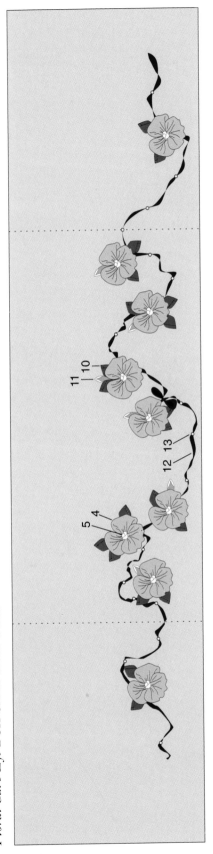

87

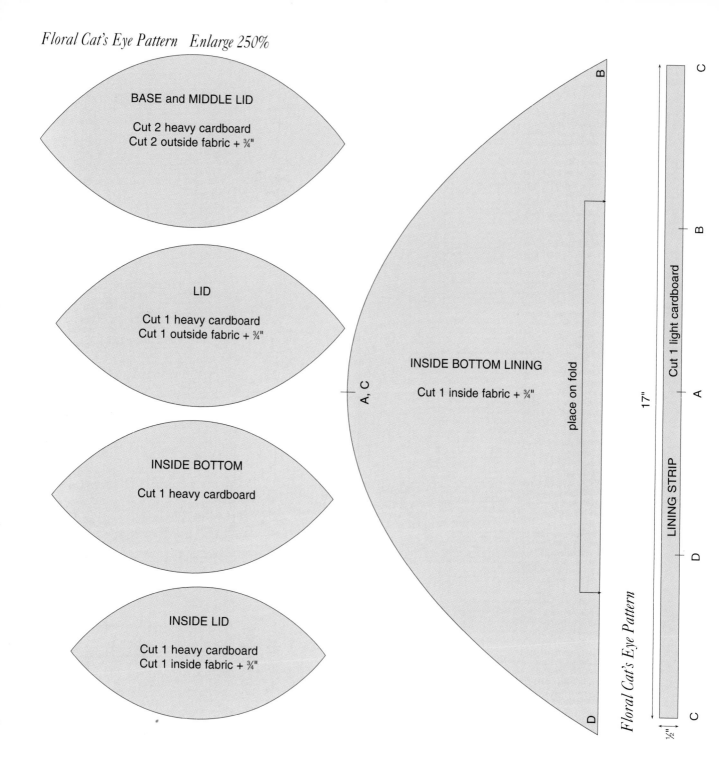

BASE and MIDDLE LID

Cut 2 heavy cardboard
Cut 2 outside fabric + ¾"

LID

Cut 1 heavy cardboard
Cut 1 outside fabric + ¾"

INSIDE BOTTOM

Cut 1 heavy cardboard

INSIDE LID

Cut 1 heavy cardboard
Cut 1 inside fabric + ¾"

INSIDE BOTTOM LINING

Cut 1 inside fabric + ¾"

place on fold

A, C

B

D

17"

LINING STRIP

Cut 1 light cardboard

C

B

A

D

C

½"

Floral Cat's Eye Pattern

There is no harvest for the heart alone, the seed of love must be Eternally resown.

—Ann Morrow Lindberg

Floral Cat's Eye Pattern

18⅞"

A

5"

Score

BOX SIDE
Cut 1 light cardboard
Cut 1 outside fabric + ¾"

8⅞"

Score

5"

4½"

Love develops deep within you. It grows, and is constantly changing.

—*Flavia*

Victorian Winter Canisters

Heavy Cardboard	Light Cardboard
BASE, INSIDE LID, and LID (Cut 3)	BOX SIDE (Cut 2 or 3 for stability)
INSIDE BOTTOM	LID STRIP (hidden by icicles)
	ICICLES and SNOW COVER: 2" x 14" (Cut 2)

Crepe Paper	Wrapping Paper
LID STRIP (hidden by icicles): 1¾" x 14½"	BOX SIDE + ¾"
ICICLES, SNOW COVER: 2½" x 15" (Cut 2)	
LID: 2½" x 20"	
INSIDE LID and BASE + ¾" (Cut 2)	
CARD RUFFLE: 1" x 20"	

Tools & Materials

For Each Box—
Heavy cardboard: 18" x 5"
Light cardboard: 20" x 30"
Crepe paper: 18" x 20" (ivory)
Wrapping paper: 13½" square (gold swirl)
Die-cut card
Stuffing

Trims: ½ yd. of ⅜"-wide (ecru lace); ½ yd. of ½"-wide (ecru lace)
Cording: ⅝ yd. of ¼"-wide (gold)
Glitter (white)
Pinecone, small

Spray sealer (clear)

Awl
Spray adhesive
Pinking shears
Drop cloth

Skaters Canister—
Trim: ½ yd. of 1⁄16"-wide (ecru/gold picot)

Father Christmas Canister—
Trim: ½ yd. of ½"-wide (ecru lace)
Silk ribbon: ¾ yd. of 7mm (dk. green)

Directions

1. Cut Cardboard and Paper

2. Form Canister and Cover with Paper

Wrap one BOX SIDE around INSIDE BOTTOM. Hold in place and squarely mark overlap. Overlap and glue one edge of BOX SIDE to opposite edge at mark. Working upside down, slip INSIDE BOTTOM into BOX SIDE. Glue in place with thin bead of glue.

Refer to Box Making Basics for Laminating on page 9 and wrap and laminate second BOX SIDE around first BOX SIDE, offsetting overlap. For a very sturdy canister, repeat with a third BOX SIDE, offsetting overlap again. This third overlap will be center back.

Mark 2¼" down from top edge at sides of BOX SIDE. Puncture ¼"-wide holes in side of box using an awl.

Laminate wrapping paper around BOX SIDE, overlapping paper at center back. Trim as necessary. Wrap excess paper to inside of box and bottom of box.

Slip cording ends through holes to inside of box. Knot ends.

3. Cover Remaining Cardboard with Paper and Glitter

Lay drop cloth on floor. Refer to Box Making Basics for Laminating Lid Strip on page 15 and laminate crepe paper to LID STRIP using spray adhesive. Glue ½" of both short edges of paper. Wrap short edges over on

91

itself at cardboard edges. Spray uncovered LID STRIP with adhesive. Wrap upper paper onto glued cardboard and smooth completely. This is outside of LID STRIP. Place on work surface outside down and roll with a 1" dowel.

Laminate crepe paper to cardboard for ICICLES and SNOW COVER using spray adhesive. Trace SNOW COVER and ICICLES patterns onto wrong side of cardboard and cut out.

Laminate crepe paper to INSIDE LID and BASE.

Puncture a ½"-diameter circle in the center of LID cardboard piece. Finger-gather while gluing LID paper to outer edge of LID cardboard. This forms a paper "cup" when turned right side up. Glue a small amount of stuffing to cupped side of LID. Unevenly pleat paper inward to center over stuffing and push excess paper through punctured hole to underside.

Place SNOW COVER piece on dropcloth and cover with light coat of spray adhesive. Coat immediately with glitter. Let dry, then shake off excess glitter. Repeat process with ICICLES, covered LID, a portion of die cut cards (Father Christmas or background tree) and pinecone. Spray with light coat of spray sealer and let dry. Place SNOW COVER on work surface wrong side up and roll with a 1" dowel. Repeat process with ICICLES.

4. Assemble and Embellish Lid

Wrap LID STRIP around INSIDE LID. Hold in place and mark overlap. Overlap and glue one short edge of LID STRIP to opposite edge at mark. Working upside down, slip INSIDE LID into LID STRIP. Glue in place with thin bead of glue, working small sections at a time and holding until glue dries. Glue extended paper over onto wrong side of INSIDE LID.

Wrap and glue straight edge of ICICLES to top edge of LID STRIP, overlapping ends at center back.

Glue edge of ⅜"-wide trim to underside edge of LID. Glue wrong side of LID to assembled lid.

Glue pinecone to center of LID. Use punctured hole in LID as a resting place for pinecone.

5. Embellish Box Bottom

Glue glittered portion of card to center front of BOX SIDE about ⅜" up from bottom edge. For Father Christmas, <u>Flute</u> while gluing silk ribbon to underside edge of some of the image, then glue in place. Glue edge of ½"-wide trim to underside edge of SNOW COVER. Cut crepe paper strip with pinking shears and finger-gather while gluing strip to underside edge of card with children. Glue child over glittered Father Christmas.

For Skaters, glue picot trim to front top edge of SNOW COVER. Wrap and glue SNOW COVER around bottom of BOX SIDE, overlapping ends at front. Cut crepe paper strip with pinking shears and finger-gather while gluing strip to underside edge of card.

Glue edge of 1"-wide lace trim to underside edge of bottom of box, slightly gathering while gluing. Glue wrong side of BASE to bottom of box.

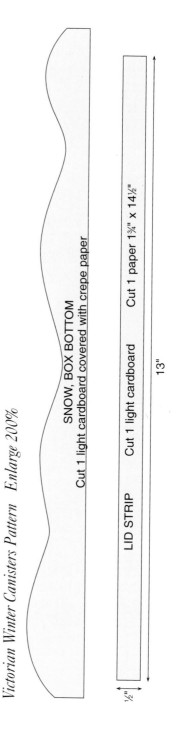

Victorian Winter Canisters Pattern   Enlarge 200%

SNOW, BOX BOTTOM
Cut 1 light cardboard covered with crepe paper

Cut 1 paper 1¾" x 14½"

LID STRIP

Cut 1 light cardboard

13"

½"

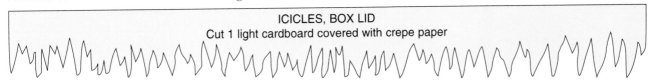

ICICLES, BOX LID
Cut 1 light cardboard covered with crepe paper

INSIDE BOTTOM

Cut 1 heavy cardboard

3⅝" circle

INSIDE LID, LID, and BASE

Cut 3 heavy cardboard
Cut 2 paper + ¾"
Cut 1 paper 2½" x 20"

3⅞" circle

Victorian Winter Canisters Pattern

12"

12"

BOX SIDE

Cut 2 light cardboard
Cut 1 gold foil + ¾"

*Love is all we have,
the only way that each
can help the other.*

—Euripides

93

Sculpted Egg & Shell Boxes

Both Boxes	
Heavy Cardboard	**Light Cardboard**
BASE	BOX SIDE
INSIDE BOTTOM	
INSIDE LID (Cut 3)	

Egg Box	
Paper	**Lace**
BOX SIDE (outside): 3" x 7¾"	INSIDE BOTTOM + ½"
BOX SIDE (inside): 1¼" x 6½"	BOX SIDE (inside and outside): about
BASE + ½"	4" x 6¾" jagged and uneven
INSIDE BOTTOM + ½"	
INSIDE LID + ¾"	
Lid liner: tear to fit	

Shell Box	
Paper	**Lace**
BOX SIDE (outside): 2½" x 8½"	BOX SIDE: 4" x 8½"
BOX SIDE (inside): 1¼" x 7¼"	
BASE + ½" + tear one slightly larger	
than BASE	
INSIDE BOTTOM + ½"	
INSIDE LID + ¾"	
Lid liner: tear to fit	

<u>Tools & Materials</u>

For Each Box—
Heavy cardboard: 9" x 4"

Industrial-strength adhesive
Corrugated cardboard: 7" x 9"
Tin foil
Embossing fluid
Sharp cutting tool (darning needle or knife)

Egg Box—
Light cardboard: 2" x 6¾"
Paper: 5" x 12" (ecru handmade)
Lace: 5" x 9" (ecru vintage)
Wire-edge ribbon: 1 yd. of ⅝"-wide (ivory)

Silk ribbon: 2 yds. of 4mm (ivory)
Trims: ⅛ yd. of 1"-wide (ecru lace with leaves);
  ⅓ yd. of 1/16"-wide (ivory picot)
Rubber stamp: egg
Modeling compound: 1 package (brilliant ivory)

Shell Box—
Light cardboard: 1½" x 7½"
Paper: 5" x 12" (burgundy handmade)
Lace: 4" x 9" (ecru vintage)
Appliqué: 1" (ecru lace)
Rubber stamp: shell
Modeling compound: 1 package each
  (pearl, brilliant ivory)

Directions

1. Cut Cardboard and Fabric or Paper

2. Stamp and Bake Lids

Prepare a clean work surface. Use tools that are not used for cooking. Cover top and bottom of corrugated cardboard with tin foil to make a baking sheet. Heat oven according to manufacturer's instructions. Open window in kitchen to avoid inhaling fumes while modeling compound is baking.

To make Egg Box lid, roll a piece of modeling compound ⅛" thick onto work surface. Very firmly stamp rubber stamp into modeling compound, making certain image is very defined. Lift off stamp. Use a large darning needle or other sharp object to cut stamped image from compound, leaving a ¹⁄₁₆" border. Roll a small ball of modeling compound and flatten on baking sheet to about 1" x ¾". Lift stamped egg off work surface and place over flattened ball. Gently shape egg around flattened ball. Repeat process for Shell Box lid using pearl modeling compound and flattening ball to a 1½" circle.

NOTE: If rubber stamps are difficult to remove from modeling compound, ink stamps with embossing fluid prior to stamping modeling compound. If a mistake is made, reroll modeling compound and try again.

Using remaining brilliant ivory modeling compound, make petals by breaking off very small pieces. Flatten pieces and mold into random petal shapes. Petal shapes can be jagged, curved, rolled, or pinched. Make five petals for Egg Box and 15 petals for Shell Box. Roll one of the petals into a center bud shape. Wrap a second petal around the first to form a rose bud. Place rose buds and petals on baking sheet with LID. Bake petals following manufacturer's directions. Check on petals every five minutes, as petals will bake more quickly than LID. Turn LID upside down halfway through baking time to evenly bake underside.

3. Prepare Ribbon for Egg Box

Thoroughly wet wire-edged ribbon. Tightly wad ribbon into a ball to wrinkle. Air or machine dry ribbon.

4. Cover Cardboard with Fabric; Shape

Glue the three INSIDE LIDs together.

Refer to Box Making Basics for <u>Laminating</u> on page 9 and, for Egg Box, laminate outside of BOX SIDE with paper. Finish all four edges. Laminate paper to inside of BOX SIDE. Laminate BASE, INSIDE BOTTOM, and

Sculpted Egg & Shell Boxes Pattern   Enlarge 200%

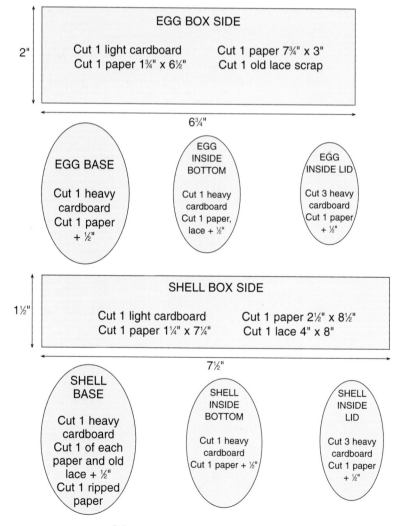

INSIDE LID with paper.

Laminate lace to INSIDE BOTTOM. Wrap edges to underside. Laminate lace to inside of BOX SIDE. Wrap jagged lace edges around and laminate to outside of BOX SIDE.

Trim lace flush to bottom and side edges of BOX SIDE. Place on work surface inside up and roll with a ½" dowel.

For Shell Box, laminate BASE and outside and inside of BOX SIDE with paper and lace. Laminate INSIDE BOTTOM, and INSIDE LID with paper. Laminate torn paper BASE to underside of BASE.

5. Assemble Box Bottom and Lid

Refer to Box Making Basics for Assembling Style B Box Side & Bottoms on page 13 and assemble BOX SIDE and INSIDE BOTTOM on both boxes.

For Egg Box, roll backside of picot trim with laminating glue. Swirl while gluing to outside of BOX SIDE. Unwrap wrinkled and dried wire-edge ribbon and cut into two equal lengths. Pull wire from one edge to gather ribbon fully. Glue gathered edge to underside edge of bottom of box. Tuck and glue cut ribbon ends to underside. Glue wrong side of BASE to bottom of box. Pull wire from one edge of remaining wire-edge ribbon piece to gather ribbon fully. Glue gathered edge to edge of torn paper lid liner, hiding cut ends. This will be wrong side of liner. Glue wrong side of liner to underside of egg LID. Glue bottom of INSIDE LID to underside of LID.

For Shell Box, glue wrong side of BASE to bottom of box. Overlap and glue petals to shelf edge of bottom of box. Glue torn paper lid liner to underside of LID. Glue bottom of INSIDE LID to underside of LID.

6. Embellish

For Egg Box, cut leaves from lace trim. Glue three leaves and two petals to center back of BOX SIDE near bottom edge. Glue one leaf and one petal to left side of BOX SIDE near bottom edge.

Glue rose bud and three lace leaves to LID. Tie two tiny bows from silk ribbon and cut ends short. Glue to petals on BOX SIDE. Cut a 12" length from silk ribbon and tie a bow. Glue bow to inside BOX SIDE at center back. Cut remaining silk ribbon in half. Hold the two lengths together as one and tie into a small bow. Glue bow to LID at base of rosebud and leaves. Knot ribbon ends and drape.

For Shell Box, glue rosebud and appliqué to LID.

China Hutch Patterns   Enlarge 200%

FRONT TRIM B
Cut 1 heavy cardboard

Cut 1 box fabric + ¾"

5³⁄₁₆"

6⁵⁄₈"

BOTTOM HALF
INSIDE BOTTOM

Cut 1 heavy cardboard
Cut 1 box fabric

True love, the gift which God has given
To man alone, beneath the heaven.
It is the secret sympathy,
The silken link, the silken tie,
Which heart to heart, and mind to mind,
In body and in soul can bind.

—Sir Walter Scott

5　Eternal Joy

Magic Box

Heavy Cardboard

LID and BASE (Cut 2)
MIDDLE LID
CENTER COMPARTMENT SIDE (Cut 3)
CENTER COMPARTMENT INSIDE
   BOTTOM (Cut 3)
OUTER COMPARTMENT SIDES (Cut 2)
OUTER COMPARTMENT INSIDE
   BOTTOM (Cut 2)
MAGIC LID INSIDE LINER (Cut 3)
MIDDLE LID OUTER EDGE (Cut 4)
BOX SIDE

Light Cardboard

MAGIC LID
MAGIC LID STRIP (Cut 3)

Moiré Fabric

BOX SIDE + ¾"
BASE + ¾"
MAGIC LID + ¾"

Satin Fabric

LID + ¾"

Lace

LID + ¾"

Silk Fabric

MIDDLE LID + ¾"
CENTER COMPARTMENT SIDE + ¾" cut 1
CENTER COMPARTMENT INSIDE BOTTOM + ½" cut 1
MAGIC LID STRIP: 6¾" x 3" (Cut 1) and 1¾" x 1" (Cut 2)
MAGIC LID INSIDE LINER + ½" (Cut 1)

Security is a sense of staying put,
but love is always in motion.

—Michael Ventura

Three Different Metallic Fabrics

from two fabrics

CENTER COMPARTMENT SIDE
   + ¾" (Cut 1 from each fabric)
CENTER COMPARTMENT INSIDE
   BOTTOM + ½" (Cut 1 from each fabric)
MAGIC LID STRIP 6¾" x 3" (Cut 1 from each fabric)
   1¾" x 1" (Cut 2 from each fabric)
MAGIC LID INSIDE LINER + ½"
   (Cut 1 from each fabric)

from third fabric

OUTER COMPARTMENT SIDE
   + ¾" (Cut 2)
OUTER COMPARTMENT INSIDE
   BOTTOM + ¾" (Cut 2)

Quilt Batting

LID (Cut 2)
CENTER COMPARTMENT INSIDE
   BOTTOM (Cut 3)

MAGIC LID INSIDE LINER (Cut 3)
OUTER COMPARTMENT INSIDE
   BOTTOM (Cut 3)

Tools & Materials

Heavy cardboard: 20" x 30"
Light cardboard: 6" x 15"
Moiré fabric: ¼ yd. (taupy gray)
Satin fabric: 5½" x 10½" (dk. gray)
Lace: 5½" x 10½" (taupy gray
  Chantilly)
Silk fabric: 22" x 9" (heather/black
  print)
Metallic fabrics: 7" x 18" (ivory),
  7" x 18" (gold), 8" x 15" (lilac)
Quilt batting: 18" x 8"

Metallic ribbon: 2 yds. of 3mm
  (silver)
Satin ribbon: 24" of ¼"-wide
  (silver)
Sheer ribbon: 1½ yds. of ½"-wide
  (black cross-dyed)
Velvet ribbon: 24" of ³⁄₁₆"-wide
  (black)
Trims: 24" of ¼"-wide (black
  beaded); 24" of ³⁄₁₆"-wide (black
  braided)
Beads: 1 package each of silver
  and charcoal seed
Charm: 1"-wide antique silver

Needle: beading
Thread: coordinating

Directions

1. Cut Cardboard and Fabric;
Score

2. Cover Cardboard with Fabric;
Shape

Refer to Box Making Basics
for <u>Laminating</u> on page 9 and
laminate scored side of BOX
SIDE with moiré fabric. Finish
one long and one short edge of
cardboard. Let dry 10 minutes.
Place wrong side up on work
surface. Fold at each score mark
and emphasize scores.

Laminate MAGIC LID with
moiré fabric. Finish all four edges.
Do not laminate BASE at this
time.

Laminate unscored side of one
CENTER COMPARTMENT
SIDE with silk fabric. Finish two
long edges and one short edge.
Place covered side up on work
surface. Fold at each score mark
and emphasize scores.

Refer to Diagram 1 and glue
two sets of two MIDDLE LID
OUTER EDGE PIECES to-
gether. Glue a set to each outer
edge of MIDDLE LID and
laminate this side of MIDDLE
LID with silk fabric.

Diagram 1

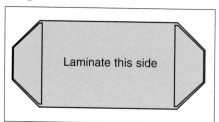

Refer to Photo 1 and laminate
the 1¾" x 1" silk fabric pieces over
score lines on one side of a
MAGIC LID STRIP. One piece
will cover the mountain score and
the second piece will cover the
valley score. Designate this side
of the cardboard as inside of
MAGIC LID STRIP. Refer to
Photo 2 and laminate the opposite
side of MAGIC LID STRIP with
silk fabric. Finish the two long
edges only. At short edges, trim
fabric flush to cardboard.
Designate this opposite side of
the cardboard as outside of
MAGIC LID STRIP. When
dry, refer to Diagram 2 and fold at
mountain and valley scores and
emphasize scores.

Photo 1

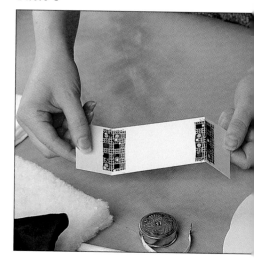

Photo 2

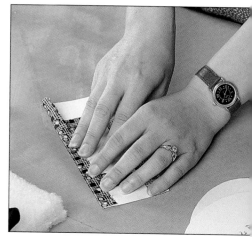

Diagram 2

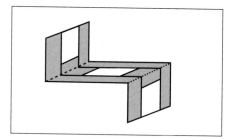

Laminate unscored side of
second CENTER COMPART-
MENT SIDE with ivory metallic
fabric. Finish two long edges and

one short edge. Repeat process on third CENTER COMPARTMENT SIDE using gold metallic fabric. Laminate the 1¾" x 1" ivory metallic pieces over score lines on a second MAGIC LID STRIP in same manner as first MAGIC LID STRIP. Finish as before. Repeat process on third MAGIC LID STRIP using gold metallic fabric.

Laminate unscored side of both OUTER COMPARTMENT SIDES with lilac metallic fabric. Finish two long edges and one short edge on each cardboard piece. Fold at each score and emphasize scores.

Refer to Box Making Basics for Padding & Wrapping on page 10 and pad LID with two layers of quilt batting, then wrap with satin fabric. Overlay and wrap lace around LID.

Pad CENTER COMPARTMENT INSIDE BOTTOMS with quilt batting, then wrap with silk fabric, ivory metallic fabric, and gold metallic fabric. Pad MAGIC LID INSIDE LINERS with quilt batting, then wrap with silk fabric, ivory metallic fabric, and gold metallic fabric.

Pad OUTER COMPARTMENT INSIDE BOTTOMS with quilt batting, then wrap with lilac metallic fabric.

3. Assemble Compartments

Join short edges of silk CENTER COMPARTMENT SIDE by overlapping tab fabric edge to finished short edge and adjoining cardboard edges together. Glue fabric tab in place. Working upside down, slip CENTER COMPARTMENT

INSIDE BOTTOM into COMPARTMENT SIDE bottom edge. Secure with a thin bead of glue, working one edge at a time. Repeat process using ivory and gold metallic CENTER COMPARTMENT SIDES and INSIDE BOTTOMS.

Join short edges of lilac metallic OUTER COMPARTMENT SIDES by overlapping tab fabric edge to finished short edge and adjoining cardboard edges together. Glue fabric tab in place. Working upside down, slip OUTER COMPARTMENT INSIDE BOTTOM into OUTER COMPARTMENT SIDE bottom edge. Secure with a thin bead of glue, working one edge at a time. Repeat process using second OUTER COMPARTMENT SIDE and INSIDE BOTTOM.

Refer to Diagram 3 and align compartment sides at longer edges in the following order: lilac metallic outer compartment, ivory metallic center compartment, silk center compartment, gold metallic center compartment, lilac metallic outer compartment. Glue sides together. Make certain top edges of compartments are lined up evenly. Thoroughly flatten glue between each compartment before proceeding.

Diagram 3

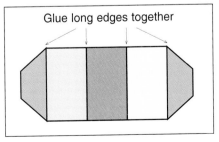
Glue long edges together

4. Assemble Magic Lid

Refer to Diagram 4 and glue wrong side of silk MAGIC LID INSIDE LINER to inside center section of MAGIC LID STRIP. Place inside liner centered between outer long edges and score lines. Repeat for remaining MAGIC LID INSIDE LINERs.

Place MAGIC LID on work surface, finished side up. Place the outside, center section of the silk MAGIC LID STRIP against the finished side of MAGIC LID at its center. One "flap" of the MAGIC LID STRIP will naturally want to wrap around to the underside of the MAGIC LID. The other "flap" will naturally fold up.

Diagram 4

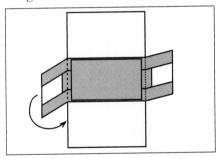

Refer to Diagram 5 and glue the "wrap around flap" to the underside of the MAGIC LID, making certain the scored edge rests snugly at the MAGIC LID edge.

Diagram 5

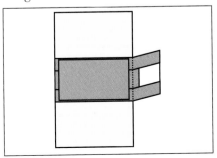

107

Refer to Diagram 6 and place the outside, center section of the ivory metallic MAGIC LID STRIP against the finished side of the MAGIC LID, adjacent and to the right of the silk piece. The flap that naturally wraps around to the underside of the MAGIC LID must be positioned on the opposite edge of the MAGIC LID than the silk strip. Line the long, outer edge of the MAGIC LID STRIP evenly with the outer, short edge of the MAGIC LID. Glue the "wrap around flap" to the underside of MAGIC LID.

Diagram 6

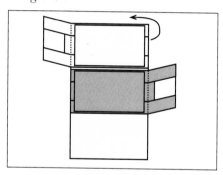

Refer to Diagram 7 and place the outside, center section of the gold metallic MAGIC LID STRIP against the finished side of MAGIC LID, adjacent and to the left of the silk piece and with the wrap around flap in the same direction as for the ivory metallic flap. Line the long, outer edge of the MAGIC LID STRIP evenly with the remaining outer short edge of the MAGIC LID. Glue the "wrap around flap" to the underside of MAGIC LID.

Diagram 7

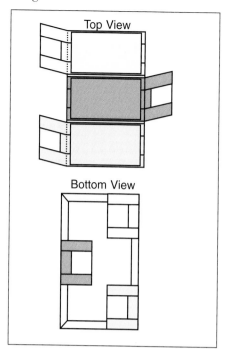

Top View

Bottom View

Refer to Diagram 8 and Photo 3 and center and place assembled MAGIC LID over the three center compartments, wrong side up. Position remaining "flaps" over the short outer sides of the center compartments. Fit and glue flaps to outer sides. The middle flap is positioned with the middle compartment on one side of the box. The two outer flaps are positioned over the outer center compartments on the opposite side of the box.

Diagram 8

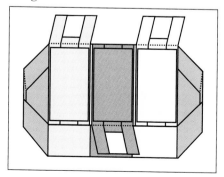

Diagram 8 (cont.)

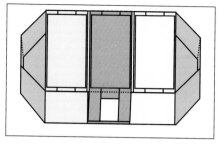

Photo 3

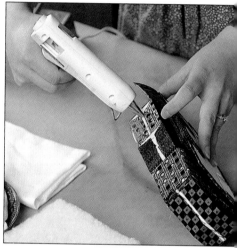

5. Finish Box Bottom

Wrap and glue wrong side of BOX SIDE to assembled compartments, over the MAGIC LID flaps. Begin with fabric tabbed edge section. Glue tab in place after first section has been glued to compartment sides. Align top edge of BOX SIDE with top edges of MAGIC LID. BOX SIDE will extend ⅛" past bottom edge of compartments. Continue to glue BOX SIDE to compartments, one section at a time, pulling BOX SIDE tight to fit. Overlap finished edge over tab edge and glue in place.

Refer to Photo 4 and wrap and glue extending fabric from bottom long edge of BOX SIDE to underside of compartments.

Photo 4

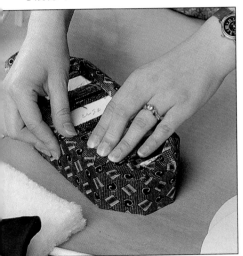

Place BASE into underside of box. Trim slightly if necessary. Laminate BASE with moiré fabric. Finish all edges. Let dry. Glue wrong side of BASE to underside of box.

Laminate velvet ribbon to bottom edge of BOX SIDE. Position beaded trim just above top edge of velvet ribbon and laminate to BOX SIDE.

6. Assemble Lid

Refer to Ribbon Placement Diagram on page 110 and crisscross metallic ribbon on LID. Glue ribbon ends to underside only. Sew silver and charcoal seed beads onto ribbon, alternating shades. Stitch charm to center of LID.

Glue wrong side of MAGIC LID to right side center section

of MIDDLE LID in between MIDDLE LID OUTER EDGE PIECES.

Laminate braided trim to underside, outer edge of MIDDLE LID/MAGIC LID.

Flute while gluing sheer ribbon to underside edge of LID.

Glue wrong side of LID to wrong side of MIDDLE LID.

Magic Box Patterns   Enlarge 200%

3⅜"

1⅞"

MAGIC LID INSIDE LINER

Cut 3 heavy cardboard
Cut 1 heather print, ivory metallic, and gold metallic + ½"
Cut 3 batting

OUTER COMPARTMENTS INSIDE BOTTOM
Cut 2 heavy cardboard
Cut 2 lilac metallic + ¾"
Cut 2 batting

3⁷⁄₁₆"

1¹⁵⁄₁₆"

CENTER COMPARTMENTS INSIDE BOTTOM

Cut 3 heavy cardboard
Cut 1 heather print, ivory metallic, and gold metallic + ½"
Cut 3 batting

MIDDLE LID OUTER EDGE
Cut 4 heavy cardboard

MIDDLE LID

Cut 1 heavy cardboard
Cut 1 heather print + ¾"

LID and BASE
(trim down for base as necessary)

Cut 2 heavy cardboard
Cut 1 moire + ¾" (base)
Cut 1 satin and lace + ¾" (lid)
Cut 2 batting

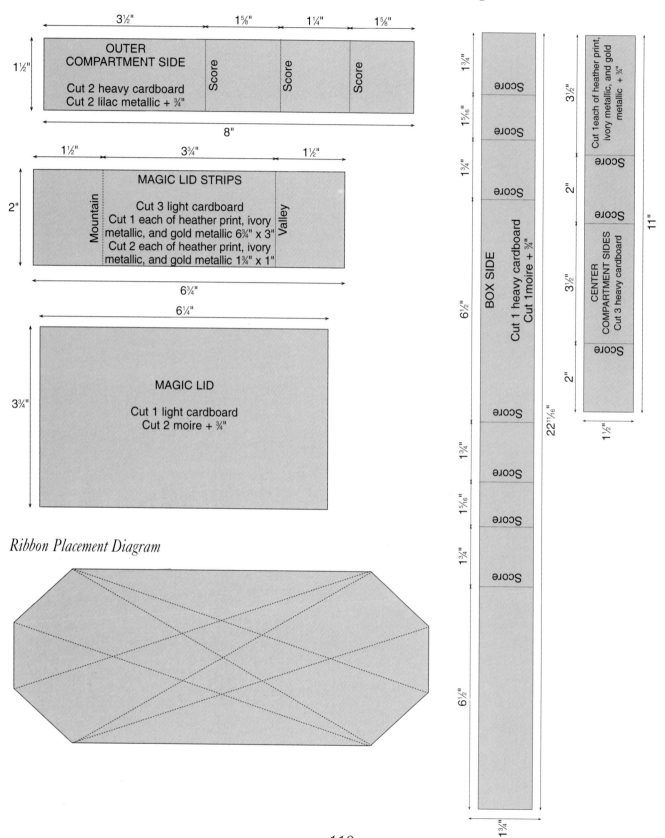

3½"   1⅝"   1¼"   1⅝"

1½"

OUTER COMPARTMENT SIDE

Score   Score   Score

Cut 2 heavy cardboard
Cut 2 lilac metallic + ¾"

8"

1½"   3¾"   1½"

2"

MAGIC LID STRIPS

Mountain

Cut 3 light cardboard
Cut 1 each of heather print, ivory
metallic, and gold metallic 6¾" x 3"
Cut 2 each of heather print, ivory
metallic, and gold metallic 1¾" x 1"

Valley

6¾"

6¼"

3¾"

MAGIC LID

Cut 1 light cardboard
Cut 2 moire + ¾"

Ribbon Placement Diagram

1¾"

Score

1⁵⁄₁₆"

Score

1¾"

Score

6½"

BOX SIDE

Cut 1 heavy cardboard
Cut 1 moire + ¾"

Score

1¾"

Score

1⁵⁄₁₆"

Score

1¾"

Score

6½"

1¾"

22¹¹⁄₁₆"

3½"

Cut 1 each of heather print,
ivory metallic, and gold
metallic + ¾"

Score

2"

Score

**CENTER
COMPARTMENT SIDES**

Cut 3 heavy cardboard

3½"

Score

2"

11"

1½"

110

The things you can prove are often not very interesting. You can't prove your love to your child or your husband or your friends. So much of life is a great and wonderful mystery.

—Madeleine L'Engel

If the sum of our unspoken admiration, love, approval, and encouragement could find expression, nine-tenths of the world's woes would be healed as if by magic.

—Margery Wilson

Oh, the miraculous energy that flows between two people who care enough to take the risks of responding with the whole heart.

—*Alex Noble*

Love Letters

Heavy Cardboard	Fabric
INSIDE BOX SIDE	INSIDE BOX SIDE + ½"
INSIDE BOTTOM & SPINE #1	INSIDE BOTTOM & SPINE + ¾"
OUTSIDE BOX SIDE	OUTSIDE BOX SIDE + ½"
SPINE #2	SPINE #2 + ½"
JACKET BACK/OUTER SPINE	JACKET BACK/OUTER SPINE and
JACKET FRONT	JACKET FRONT: 11½" x 7½",
INSIDE LID	+ 5⅞" x 1½" strip
JACKET FRONT RAISED SECTION	INSIDE LID + ¾"
(Cut 2)	

Tools & Materials

Heavy cardboard: 11" x 30"
Fabric: ¼ yd. of 44"-wide
(natural white linen)

Lace: 5½" x 11" (natural white
vintage)
Velvet ribbon: ½ yd. of ³⁄₁₆"-
wide (ivory)
Silk ribbon: 1 yd. of 13mm
(natural white)
Trim: ¼ yd. of ½"-wide (ivory
lace)
Die-cut card: 5" x 3½"

Directions

1. Cut Cardboard and Fabric;
Score

2. Cover Cardboard with Fabric;
Shape
  Refer to Box Making Basics
for <u>Laminating</u> on page 9 and
laminate unscored side of
INSIDE BOX SIDE with fabric.
Finish the two long edges only.
  Laminate unscored side of
INSIDE BOTTOM & SPINE
with fabric. Finish all four edges.
Let dry. Place covered side up on
work surface. Fold on score line

to emphasize score. Roll SPINE
#1 section with a 1" dowel.
Because this is heavy cardboard, it
is not as easy to roll as lightweight
cardboard. Keep working with it
until ridges have been eliminated.
  Laminate scored side of
OUTSIDE BOX SIDE with
fabric. Finish the two long edges
only.
  Laminate SPINE #2 with
fabric. Finish all four edges. Let
dry. Place wrong side up on work
surface and roll with a 1" dowel.
  Laminate INSIDE LID with
fabric. Finish all four edges.
  Glue the two JACKET
FRONT RAISED SECTIONS
together, then glue to JACKET
FRONT, ¼" from outer edges and
¾" from top edge.
  Refer to Diagram 1 and
laminate scored side of JACKET
BACK & OUTER SPINE and
raised section side of JACKET
FRONT with fabric, positioning
JACKET BACK & OUTER
SPINE ¾" from short edge and
leaving a ¹⁄₁₆" space between
straight edges of JACKET BACK
& OUTER SPINE and JACKET
FRONT. This becomes the BOX

JACKET. Smooth fabric to
cardboard and all around raised
section on BOX JACKET. Do not
finish edges at this time.
  Place BOX JACKET covered
side down on work surface.
Laminate fabric strip over gap
between JACKET FRONT and
JACKET BACK & OUTER
SPINE. Finish all four edges of
BOX JACKET. Clip fabric at
rounded corners. Let Dry. Place
BOX JACKET wrong side up on
work surface. Fold on score lines
and emphasize scores. Roll
OUTER SPINE section with a 1"
dowel.

Diagram 1

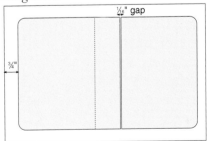

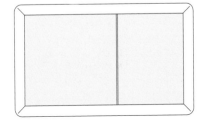

3. Assemble and Embellish Box Bottom

Working upside down, place a thin bead of glue along outer, long edge of INSIDE BOTTOM. Place glued edge on edge of INSIDE BOX SIDE center section. Hold until glue dries. Glue short edges of INSIDE BOTTOM to short edges of INSIDE BOX SIDE. Where curves meet SPINE #1, glue extended fabric from INSIDE BOX SIDE over onto wrong side of SPINE #1, adjoining cardboard edges together.

<u>Flute</u> while gluing silk ribbon to underside top edge of assembled box bottom.

Glue wrong side of SPINE #2 to wrong side of SPINE #1, aligning bottom edges.

Wrap and glue wrong side of OUTSIDE BOX SIDE to wrong side of INSIDE BOX SIDE, aligning bottom edges. Where curves meet SPINE #2, glue extended fabric from OUTSIDE BOX SIDE over onto wrong side of SPINE #2, adjoining cardboard edges together. Glue trim over seams.

Glue velvet ribbon to bottom edge of OUTSIDE BOX SIDE. Wrap ribbon ends onto SPINE #2.

4. Assemble Jacket

Place and glue box bottom and spine into inside of BOX JACKET so inner spine is snug against outer spine and BOX JACKET closes easily.

Glue edge of trim to underside front edge of INSIDE LID. Center and glue wrong side of INSIDE LID to inside of JACKET FRONT.

Laminate lace to outside of BOX JACKET.

Laminate die-cut card to INSIDE LID.

Love Letters Patterns   Enlarge 200%

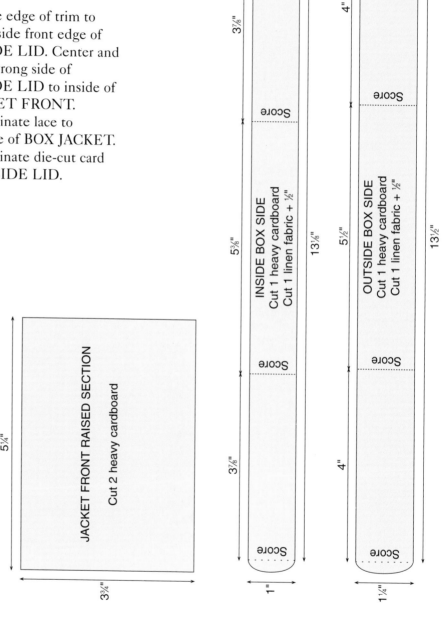

JACKET FRONT RAISED SECTION

Cut 2 heavy cardboard

5¼"

3¾"

INSIDE BOX SIDE
Cut 1 heavy cardboard
Cut 1 linen fabric + ½"

Score

Score

Score

Score

3⅞"

5⅜"

13⅛"

3⅞"

1"

OUTSIDE BOX SIDE
Cut 1 heavy cardboard
Cut 1 linen fabric + ½"

Score

Score

Score

Score

4"

5½"

13½"

4"

1¼"

Keep love in your life, my friend,
If you would have perfect joy.

—Thomas Curtis Clark

114

Love Letters Patterns   Enlarge 200%

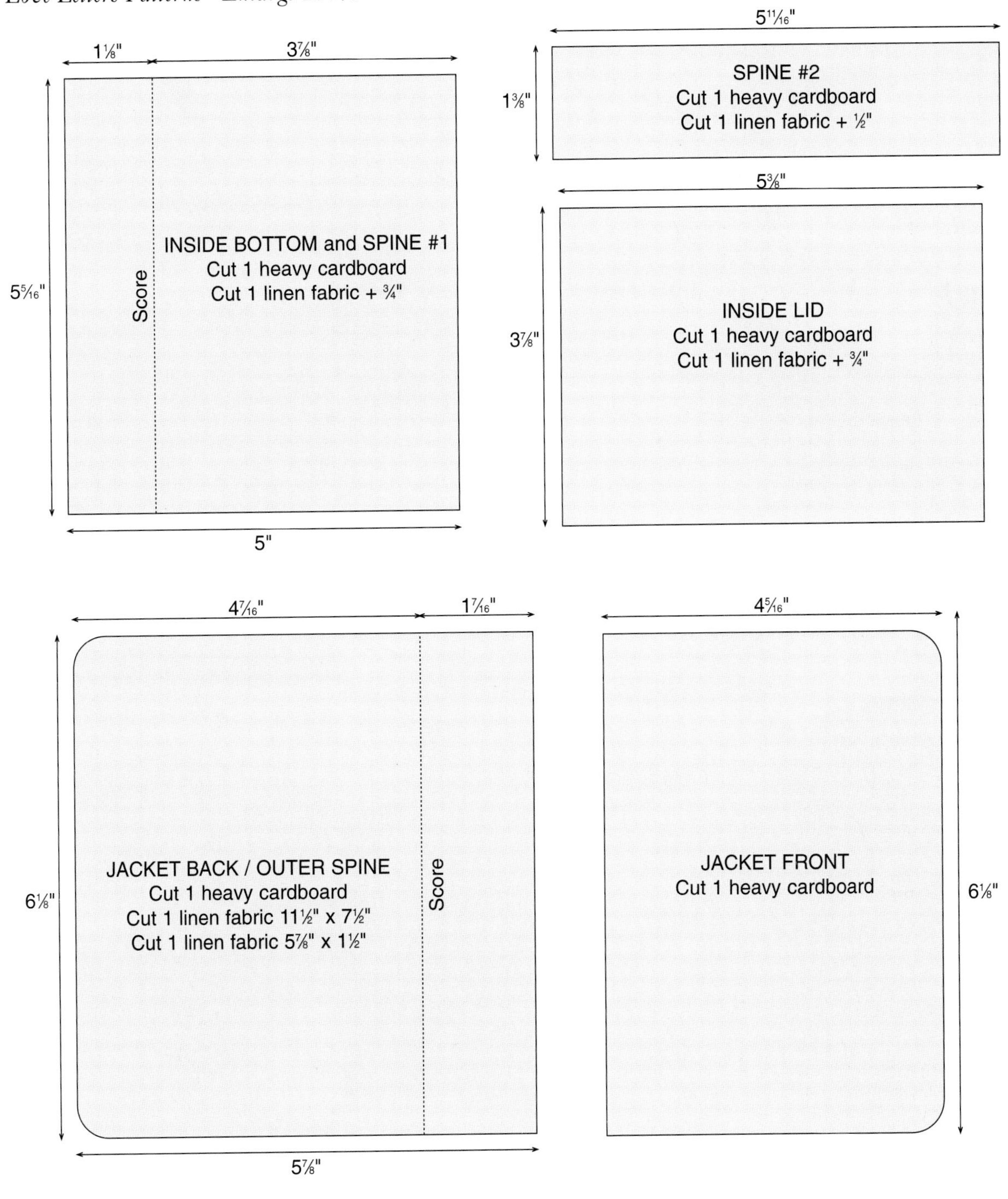
1⅛"
3⅞"
5⁵⁄₁₆"
INSIDE BOTTOM and SPINE #1
Cut 1 heavy cardboard
Cut 1 linen fabric + ¾"
Score
5"
5¹¹⁄₁₆"
1⅜"
SPINE #2
Cut 1 heavy cardboard
Cut 1 linen fabric + ½"
5⅜"
3⅞"
INSIDE LID
Cut 1 heavy cardboard
Cut 1 linen fabric + ¾"
4⁷⁄₁₆"
1⁷⁄₁₆"
6⅛"
JACKET BACK / OUTER SPINE
Cut 1 heavy cardboard
Cut 1 linen fabric 11½" x 7½"
Cut 1 linen fabric 5⅞" x 1½"
Score
5⅞"
4⁵⁄₁₆"
JACKET FRONT
Cut 1 heavy cardboard
6⅛"

For love is a celestial harmony of likely hearts composed of stars' consent,
which join together in sweet sympathy, to work each other's joy and true content.

—*Edmund Spencer*

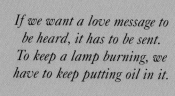

*If we want a love message to
be heard, it has to be sent.
To keep a lamp burning, we
have to keep putting oil in it.*

—Mother Teresa

*When I send thee a red,
red rose,
The sweetest flower on
earth that grows!
Think, dear heart, how I
love thee; . . . .*

—Friedrich Ruckert

Ivy Box

Heavy Cardboard	Light Cardboard
BASE	INSIDE BOTTOM LIP STRIP
INSIDE BOTTOM	OUTSIDE BOTTOM LIP STRIP
INSIDE LID	LID STRIP
LID RIM	

Mylar	Fabric
BOX SIDE	BASE + ½"
LID	INSIDE BOTTOM + ½"
	INSIDE LID + ⅜"
	LID STRIP + ½"
	INSIDE BOTTOM LIP STRIP + ½"
	OUTSIDE BOTTOM LIP STRIP + ½"

Tools & Materials

Heavy cardboard: 7" x 30"
Light cardboard: 3" x 30"
Mylar: 5" x 30"
Fabric: ¼ yd. of 44"-54"-wide (ivory jacquard)
Sponge: small holed

Suede ribbon: 3 yds. of 1"-wide (dk. green)
Sheer ribbon: 1½ yds. of 9mm (tan)
Textured ribbon: 1½ yds. of 7mm (dk. green cross-dyed)
Trim: ¾ yd. of ½"-wide (metallic gold braid)
Rubber stamp: ivy
Ink pad (dk. green)
Embossing powder (clear)
Glass paints (gold sparkle, green)

What is the beginning? Love.
What is the course? Love still.
What the goal? The goal is Love
on the happy hill.
Is there nothing then but Love?
Search we sky or earth,
There is nothing out of Love
Hath perpetual worth:
All things flag but only Love,
All things fail and flee;
There is nothing left but Love,
Worthy you and me.

—Christina Rossetti

Directions

1. Cut Cardboard, Fabric, and Mylar

2. Stamp and Emboss Mylar BOX SIDE and LID, and Paint
  Refer to Box Making Basics for Stamping & Embossing on page 21 and center and stamp ivy onto BOX SIDE , then immediately emboss. Repeat process on LID and around BOX SIDE, evenly spacing stamps.
  Pour green glass paint onto a palette. Load sponge with very little paint. Bounce sponge tip on a paper towel and then lightly over each stamped impression on BOX SIDE and LID.
  Pour gold sparkle glass paint onto a palette. Lightly Stipple paint over entire BOX SIDE and LID, except on stamped impressions. Let dry.

3. Cover Cardboard with Fabric and Ribbon; Shape
  Refer to Box Making Basics for Laminating on page 9 and laminate BASE and INSIDE BOTTOM with fabric. Laminate INSIDE LID with fabric, beginning with outer edge. Cut out fabric from center of LID to within ¾" of cardboard. Clip curves as necessary and complete lamination.

118

Laminate INSIDE BOTTOM LIP STRIP, OUTSIDE BOTTOM LIP STRIP, and LID STRIP with fabric. Finish all four edges. Place INSIDE BOTTOM LIP STRIP finished side up on work surface and roll with a 1" dowel. Place OUTSIDE BOTTOM LIP STRIP and LID STRIP wrong side up on work surface and roll with a 1" dowel.

Diagonally wrap LID RIM with suede ribbon. Designate one side of cardboard as underside and begin gluing end of ribbon to underside. Wrap ribbon around entire LID RIM.

4. Assemble Box Bottom

Wrap right side of INSIDE BOTTOM LIP STRIP around INSIDE BOTTOM. Mark overlap and glue. With wrong side up, slip INSIDE BOTTOM into assembled INSIDE BOTTOM LIP STRIP at top edge. Glue in place on underside with a thick bead of glue. The inside bottom of the box sits ½" up from the base because the mylar BOX SIDE must have a surface to rest against. Cut several layers from scrap cardboard to fit into the underside of assembled inside bottom and glue in place.

Wrap BOX SIDE around outer edge of INSIDE BOTTOM LIP STRIP. Glue overlap using industrial strength adhesive and hold in place with clothespins until glue dries. Slip BOX SIDE over INSIDE BOTTOM LIP STRIP. Glue bottom edge of BOX SIDE to outer INSIDE BOTTOM LIP STRIP using industrial strength adhesive. Let dry.

Wrap wrong side of OUTSIDE BOTTOM LIP STRIP around BASE. Mark overlap and glue. With wrong side up, slip BASE into assembled OUTSIDE BOTTOM LIP STRIP at bottom edge. Glue in place on underside with a thick bead of glue.

Slip assembled base/outside lip strip over BOX SIDE and glue together on underside of inside bottom.

Laminate suede ribbon to OUTSIDE BOTTOM LIP STRIP so one long ribbon edge is aligned with top edge of OUTSIDE BOTTOM LIP STRIP. Glue extending ribbon to bottom of box.

Laminate trim over top edge of OUTSIDE BOTTOM LIP STRIP.

5. Assemble Lid; Embellish

Assemble INSIDE LID/LID STRIP in the same manner as BASE/OUTSIDE BOTTOM LIP STRIP.

Laminate suede ribbon to outside of LID STRIP, aligning one long ribbon edge to bottom edge of LID STRIP. Glue extending ribbon over onto wrong side of INSIDE LID.

Glue mylar LID to wrong side of assembled lid with industrial strength adhesive. Let dry.

Flute while gluing sheer ribbon to underside inner edge of LID RIM. Flute while gluing textured ribbon to underside outer edge of LID RIM.

With wrong sides together, glue LID RIM to INSIDE LID.

*It is as if, in the complex
language of love,
there were a word that
could only be spoken by
lips when lips touch,
a silent contract sealed
with a kiss.*

—Diane Ackerman

*Love is everything it's
cracked up to be. That's
why people are so cynical
about it. It really is worth
fighting for, being brave
for, risking everything for.
And the trouble is, if you
don't risk anything, you
risk even more.*

—Erica Jong

Ivy Box Patterns

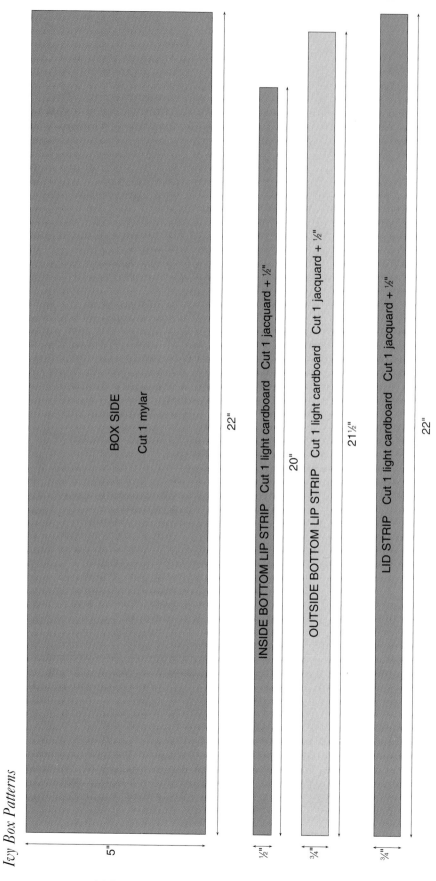

BOX SIDE

Cut 1 mylar

5"

22"

INSIDE BOTTOM LIP STRIP   Cut 1 light cardboard   Cut 1 jacquard + ½"

½"

20"

OUTSIDE BOTTOM LIP STRIP   Cut 1 light cardboard   Cut 1 jacquard + ½"

¾"

21½"

LID STRIP   Cut 1 light cardboard   Cut 1 jacquard + ½"

¾"

22"

120

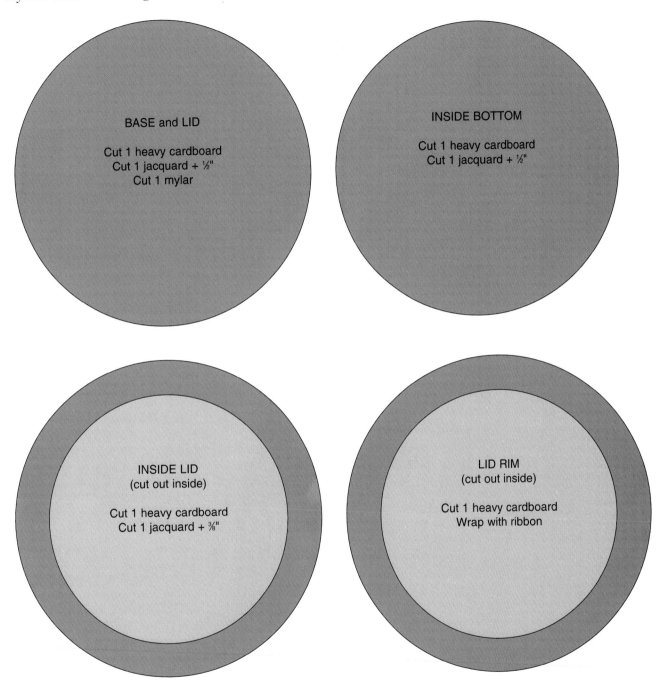

BASE and LID

Cut 1 heavy cardboard
Cut 1 jacquard + ½"
Cut 1 mylar

INSIDE BOTTOM

Cut 1 heavy cardboard
Cut 1 jacquard + ½"

INSIDE LID
(cut out inside)

Cut 1 heavy cardboard
Cut 1 jacquard + ⅜"

LID RIM
(cut out inside)

Cut 1 heavy cardboard
Wrap with ribbon

Love is the river of life in this world. Think not that ye know it who stand at the little tinkling rill, the first small fountain. Not until you have gone through the rocky gorges, and not lost the stream; not until you have gone through the meadow, and the stream has widened and deepened until fleets could ride on its bosom; not until beyond the meadow you have come to the the unfathomable ocean, and poured your treasures into its depths—not until then can you know what love is.

—Henry Ward Beecher

Garden Bouquet

Heavy Cardboard	Light Cardboard	Quilt Batting
BASE and MIDDLE LID (Cut 2) LID INSIDE BOTTOM INSIDE LID (Cut 3)	BOX SIDE LINING STRIP	LID (Cut 2) INSIDE BOTTOM INSIDE LID

Moiré Fabric	Over-printed Jacquard Fabric	Silk Fabric
BOX SIDE + ¾" LID: 5½" x 7¼"	BASE and MIDDLE LID + ¾" (Cut 2)	INSIDE BOTTOM LINING INSIDE LID + ¾"

Tools & Materials
Heavy cardboard: 30" x 7"
Light cardboard: 3" x 15"
Moiré fabric: 9" x 15" (dk. ecru)
Jacquard fabric: 6" x 14" (black/tan)
Silk fabric: 9" x 12" (dusty aqua)
Quilt batting: 6" x 12"

Velvet ribbon: 1¼ yds. of ³⁄₁₆"-wide (burgundy)
Wire-edge ribbon: ¾ yd. of ⅝"-wide (burgundy)
Textured ribbons: ½ yd. of 3mm (metallic aqua);
   1¼ yds. of 7mm (green cross-dyed)
Silk ribbons, 4mm: ¾ yd. (dk. burgundy),
   2 yds. (khaki gold), 1¼ yds. (sea green),
   1¼ yds. (dk. sea green), 1¼ yds. (dk. red),
   ¾ yd. (rose), ¾ yd. (deep rose), ½ yd. (neutral rose),
   2 yds. (taupe)
Embroidery floss: 1 yd. (olive green), 1 yd.
   (variegated olive green)
Wool floss: 1½ yds. (variegated burgundy)

Needles: size 20 chenille; size 7 embroidery

Directions
1. Cut Cardboard and Fabric; Score

2. Embroider LID fabric
   Trace LID onto wrong side of LID fabric. Baste-stitch on traced line. Enlarge Garden Bouquet Transfer Diagram on page 126 and transfer to right side of fabric. Embroider fabric following Garden Bouquet Stitch Guide on pages 124 and 126.

Special Ribbonwork Instructions: For Knotted & Looped Ribbon Stitches, knot ribbon ¼" from entry point before completing stitch.

Description	Silk Ribbon/Floss	Stitch
1. Mum stems	variegated olive green floss (2 strands)	Outline Stitch
2. Vine stems	olive green floss (2 strands)	Outline Stitch
3. Dark rose mum (bottom)	deep rose ribbon	Knotted & Looped Ribbon Stitch
4. Dark rose mum (middle)	rose ribbon	Knotted & Looped Ribbon Stitch
5. Dark rose mum (center)	neutral rose ribbon	Knotted & Looped Ribbon Stitch
6. Pale rose half mum (bottom)	neutral rose ribbon	Knotted & Looped Ribbon Stitch
7. Pale rose half mum (middle)	rose ribbon	Knotted & Looped Ribbon Stitch
8. Pale rose half mum (top)	taupe ribbon	Knotted & Looped Ribbon Stitch
9. Gold half mums (bottom for two mums, top for third)	khaki gold ribbon	Knotted & Looped Ribbon Stitch
10. Gold half mums (bottom for one, top for other)	taupe ribbon	Knotted & Looped Ribbon Stitch
11. Dark red mum (bottom)	deep red ribbon	Knotted & Looped Ribbon Stitch
12. Dark red mum (middle)	deep burgundy ribbon	Knotted & Looped Ribbon Stitch
13. Dark red mum (center)	taupe ribbon	Knotted & Looped Ribbon Stitch
14. Vine flowers	variegated wool floss (2 strands)	Lazy Daisy
15. Dark leaves	dark sea green ribbon	Lazy Daisy
16. Light leaves	sea green ribbon	One-twist Ribbon Stitch
17. Buds	khaki gold ribbon	Cross-over Lazy Daisy
18. Buds	deep red ribbon	Cross-over Lazy Daisy

3. Cover Cardboard with Fabric; Shape

Make certain to label sections on scored side of BOX SIDE with appropriate letters. Label INSIDE BOTTOM with appropriate letters.

Refer to Box Making Basics for <u>Laminating</u> on page 9 and laminate unscored side of BOX SIDE with moiré fabric. Finish all four edges. Laminate BASE and MIDDLE LID with wrong side of jacquard fabric.

Place BOX SIDE on work surface, right side up. Fold at each score line to emphasize shape. Place on work surface, wrong side up, and roll with a ½" dowel.

Trim embroidered LID fabric ¾" beyond stitching. Refer to Box Making Basics for <u>Padding & Wrapping</u> on page 10 and pad LID with two layers of quilt batting, then wrap with moiré fabric. Clip fabric at scallop indents when wrapping fabric.

Remove baste stitching.

Glue the three INSIDE LIDS together. Pad INSIDE LID with quilt batting, then wrap with silk fabric.

4. Assemble Box Bottom

Working upside down, glue INSIDE BOTTOM section B to BOX SIDE section B. Place INSIDE BOTTOM ⅛₆" down from bottom edge of BOX SIDE. Hold in place until glue dries.

At bottom edge, glue INSIDE

BOTTOM section C to BOX SIDE section C. Hold in place until glue dries. Continue gluing matching sections of INSIDE BOTTOM and BOX SIDE together. To complete, glue finished edge of BOX SIDE section A over tabbed edge of BOX SIDE section H before gluing to INSIDE BOTTOM.

Emphasize scalloped shape by molding with fingers at curves and pinching at dips.

Glue metallic aqua textured ribbon over each scallop indent on BOX SIDE. Place glue on inside of BOX SIDE and bottom of box only.

5. Line Box Bottom; Assemble Lid

Refer to Box Making Basics for Lining Boxes on page 13 and line box.

Beginning at center front of box, glue center of LINING STRIP to top inside edge of BOX SIDE, with strip placed a scant ¹⁄₁₆" down from top edge. Finish gluing LINING STRIP to top inside edge of BOX SIDE.

Flute while gluing velvet ribbon to underside edge of LID. Glue wrong side of LID to wrong side of MIDDLE LID. Glue wrong side of INSIDE LID to right side of MIDDLE LID.

6. Finishing

Flute while gluing green cross-dyed textured ribbon to under-side edge of box bottom.

Measure and mark eight 1⅞"-intervals along wire-edge ribbon. Sew a gather stitch across width of ribbon at each mark. Gather ribbon as tightly as possible at each mark and knot thread. Trim ribbon ends to within ⅛" of stitching. Glue gathered section of ribbon to indented portion of each scallop.

Cut four 5" lengths from both taupe and khaki gold silk ribbon. Stitch a Rosette with each length. Glue alternating shades of rosettes over each gathered ribbon section, hiding stitching and raw ends.

Glue wrong side of BASE to bottom of box.

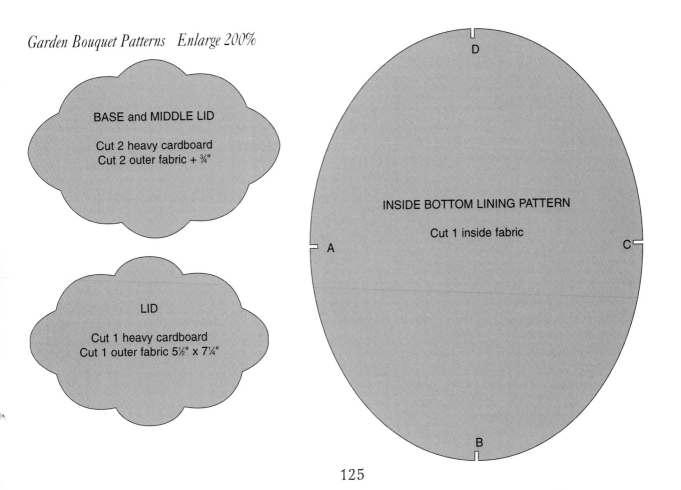

Garden Bouquet Patterns   Enlarge 200%

BASE and MIDDLE LID

Cut 2 heavy cardboard
Cut 2 outer fabric + ¾"

LID

Cut 1 heavy cardboard
Cut 1 outer fabric 5½" x 7¼"

D

INSIDE BOTTOM LINING PATTERN

Cut 1 inside fabric

A

C

B

Garden Bouquet Patterns   Enlarge 200%

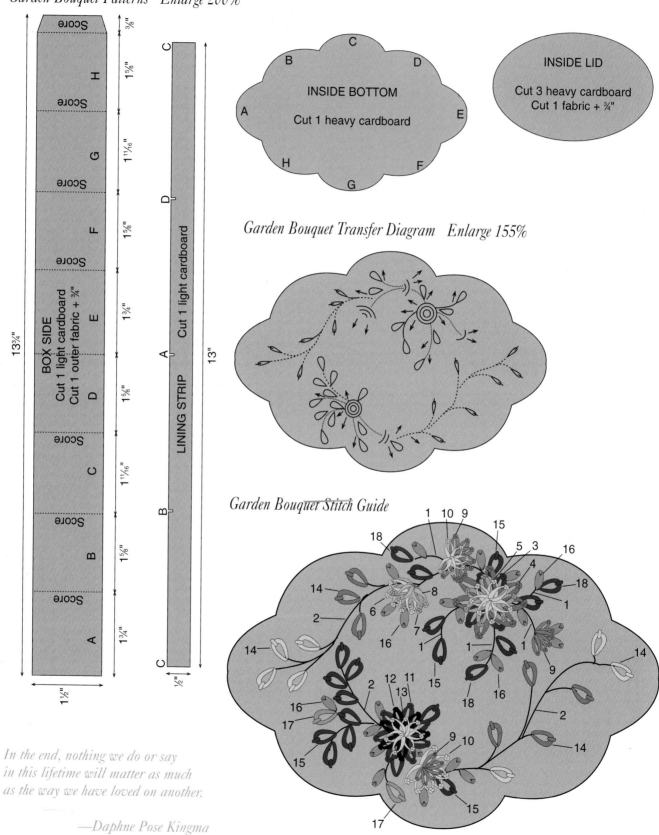

BOX SIDE
Cut 1 light cardboard
Cut 1 outer fabric + ¾"

Score   Score   Score   Score   Score   Score   Score

H   G   F   E   D   C   B   A

³⁄₈"   1⅝"   1¹¹⁄₁₆"   1⅝"   1¾"   1⅝"   1¹¹⁄₁₆"   1⅝"   1¾"

13¾"

1½"

LINING STRIP
Cut 1 light cardboard

C   D   A   B   C

13"

½"

INSIDE BOTTOM

Cut 1 heavy cardboard

C
B   D
A   E
H   F
G

INSIDE LID

Cut 3 heavy cardboard
Cut 1 fabric + ¾"

Garden Bouquet Transfer Diagram   Enlarge 155%

Garden Bouquet Stitch Guide

In the end, nothing we do or say
in this lifetime will matter as much
as the way we have loved on another.

—Daphne Pose Kingma

126

Dedication

To Alexis Megan, to mark
and celebrate the occasion
of your first love.

*Honor all the memories, from the first
butterflies to the heart-breaking good-
byes, to the hilarious final moment when
you let go (a vision forever locked in my
mind). Learn your lessons well, because
surviving difficult times teaches
perseverance. Perseverance brings about
proven character and proven character,
hope, and HOPE cannot disappoint.*

—Mom

Metric Conversion Chart

mm-millimetres   cm-centimetres
inches to millimetres and centimetres

inches	mm	cm	inches	cm	inches	cm
⅛	3	0.3	9	22.9	30	76.2
¼	6	0.6	10	25.4	31	78.7
½	13	1.3	12	30.5	33	83.8
⅝	16	1.6	13	33.0	34	86.4
¾	19	1.9	14	35.6	35	88.9
⅞	22	2.2	15	38.1	36	91.4
1	25	2.5	16	40.6	37	94.0
1¼	32	3.2	17	43.2	38	96.5
1½	38	3.8	18	45.7	39	99.1
1¾	44	4.4	19	48.3	40	101.6
2	51	5.1	20	50.8	41	104.1
2½	64	6.4	21	53.3	42	106.7
3	76	7.6	22	55.9	43	109.2
3½	89	8.9	23	58.4	44	111.8
4	102	10.2	24	61.0	45	114.3
4½	114	11.4	25	63.5	46	116.8
5	127	12.7	26	66.0	47	119.4
6	152	15.2	27	68.6	48	121.9
7	178	17.8	28	71.1	49	124.5
8	203	20.3	29	73.7	50	127.0

Index